WORKING IN
JOURNALISM

D1741883

Starting Out...

WORKING IN JOURNALISM

Elizabeth Wilson

Northcote House

© Copyright 1997 by Elizabeth Wilson

First Published in 1997 by Northcote House Publishers Ltd, Plymbridge House, Estover Road, Plymouth PL6 7PY, United Kingdom. Tel: Plymouth (01752) 202368. Fax: (01752) 202330.

British Cataloguing-in-Publication Data.
A catalogue record for this book is available from the British Library.

ISBN 0-7463-0683-0
Typeset by PDQ Typesetting, Stoke-on-Trent
Printed and bound in the United Kingdom

Contents

Acknowledgements

With thanks to the colleagues who agreed to feature herein and the organisations who provided information and allowed reproduction of their material, in particular the Press Complaints Commission and the National Union of Journalists.

Preface

'Daily journalism may be the first rough draft of history, but it doesn't seem like history at all as the stretching days of deadlines pound by. You're not paid to weave events into an enduring tapestry. You're there to anticipate and react.'
Peter Preston, editor-in-chief, *The Guardian* and *The Observer*, writing in the *Evening Standard*

'How is the world ruled and how do wars start? Diplomats tell lies to journalists and then believe what they read.'
Karl Kraus (1874–1922)

WHY WOULD ANYONE WANT TO BE A JOURNALIST?

Take the downside first. Journalism is a profession that has been the butt of **criticism** since it began. The Russian writer Leo Tolstoy called it 'an intellectual brothel'. The Labour politician Aneurin Bevan once said he read the newspapers avidly. The sting in the tail came when he added: 'It is my one form of continuous fiction.'

In more recent times, newspapers have been accused of misrepresentation, 'chequebook journalism' and invading privacy. Television journalists get accused of bias against politicians or their parties, or of being too aggressive when interviewing them. In the first half of the 1990s, politicians and the royal family waged an almost continual war against the Press, complaining of invasions of privacy. Personalities from the worlds of entertainment and sport joined the chorus.

Sometimes the criticism is justified, sometimes not. Even journalists have fostered their own poor public image by referring to themselves as 'hacks'. The dictionary defines that term as a 'literary drudge'.

Continuing the downside, the **lifestyle** of a journalist is not an

9

easy one. If you want a nine-to-five job, it is not for you. Unsocial hours are part of the job, as are unpleasant tasks like asking questions of people who have been recently bereaved and putting many hours into work which ends up on the 'spike' or the cutting room floor.

There is a more serious drawback. The journalist who ventures into a war zone or a riot faces severe danger. Some have been injured, felled by a stray bullet, others killed.

Now the **upside**. Journalism can be very attractive as a career. Why? The journalist is at the **forefront of world events** – a major disaster, a Prime Minster resigning, a financial scandal exposed.

It is not only national newspaper journalists and television reporters who scoop the big stories; local newspapers and broadcasting are just as stimulating and provide their own share of exclusives, many of which go on to be reported nationally.

The job itself is a challenge no matter whether it is for a small weekly newspaper or for the BBC's *Nine O'Clock News*. Whoever you work for, it is a matter of investigating what happened and why, and communicating that to a wider audience.

Journalism can be financially rewarding, can involve travel, and can bring you into contact with many different and fascinating cultures and people.

There are many **opportunities** for employment. There is an extensive media in Britain, from newspapers and magazines to television and radio stations, all of whom need journalists. The media is expanding and that is likely to continue. The number of television channels will grow dramatically with the advent of 'digital' transmission and the development of cable and satellite, and there will be new radio stations. New magazines are launched several times a year and, although newspapers are finding it tough to maintain profits, launches do still take place.

English-speaking journalists can also **work abroad**. There are a large number of English-language publications around the world, including Australia, the United States and the Middle East. British journalists work on these publications, as well as working abroad as a staff correspondent for the British media or as a freelance.

On the upside, too, is journalism's new **image**. In the past half decade it has cleaned up its act and put more emphasis on ethical behaviour. Tabloid newspapers have raised their standards of accuracy. Journalism is increasingly seen as a 'profession', rather than as a craft or trade.

WHAT QUALITIES WILL YOU NEED?

- Curiosity.
- The ability to express yourself clearly and concisely.
- An interest in current events of every kind.
- A wide general knowledge.
- A willingness to learn.
- Possibly most important, the gift of talking to people.

Working as a news reporter also demands courage, stamina and a thick skin. You must be able to work well under pressure because in all media, deadlines are constantly approaching. You will also need tact when dealing with people who don't want to speak to you.

You will have to develop the ability to recognise when and where a story exists, as well as the determination to root it out.

Getting a foothold in journalism means beating stiff competition. It may be easier if you have a degree. A survey in late 1994 showed that 68 per cent of journalism trainees on regional and local papers were graduates. (*Source*: Centre for Journalism Studies, Cardiff University.) However, it is certainly not essential and some editors of provincial papers have turned against the trend to recruit graduates, preferring to take on local school-leavers.

WHAT ABOUT TRAINING?

Traditionally, journalism was learned 'on the job' during a period contracted to a local newspaper. This was changing in the early 1990s, with more journalists taking college and university courses in media studies before finding employment.

As with getting a job, competition for obtaining a place on a journalism course is fierce. In 1993, the most oversubscribed courses at higher education establishments were those in the field of mass communication, with more than 20 applicants for every place. (*Source*: Universities and Colleges Admissions Service.)

But knowing what course tutors and editors look for is half the battle. If you can show a commitment to journalism, a good knowledge of world events, experience on a school newspaper or hospital radio station and boundless enthusiasm, you will be on your way.

WHERE WILL A CAREER IN JOURNALISM TAKE YOU?

Almost anywhere you want to go. Journalists commonly become

television pundits, move into politics and write books. Many combine several strands; for example, Martyn Lewis reads the news on television while becoming a successful author; Richard Littlejohn presents a television show while writing a column for the *Daily Mail*; Julie Burchill, now a successful freelance, writes best-selling novels.

The top jobs are open to all. Georgina Henry, deputy editor of *The Guardian*, began as a reporter on the magazine *Marketing Week*; Piers Morgan, editor of the *Daily Mirror*, started out in local newspapers, as did Sybil Ruscoe, the Radio 5 presenter.

If you decide journalism is for you, congratulations. It is a fascinating and worthwhile career. As the playwright Arthur Miller said: 'A good newspaper is a nation talking to itself.'

Elizabeth Wilson

1

Working in the Media

WHAT DO JOURNALISTS DO?

'In the end you're asking the question that most people want to hear asked, not to sound clever or make some grand point that can be picked up by some columnist. They're sitting at breakfast or driving their cars to work and they want you to ask the question they would if they could: Why?'
James Naughtie, presenter, *Today*, Radio 4 (*The Independent*)

'What we want are reporters who go to an event briefed on one story and return with six more because they have tuned in and picked up on conversations. We won't get them if they don't get out and involved in the community or if their circle of social contacts does not extend beyond fellow journalists.'
Rachael Campey, editor, *Express & Echo*, Exeter.
(*UK Press Gazette*)

There are about 35,000 journalists at work in Britain today. No two have jobs that are exactly the same yet there is a basic similarity; they seek out information and convey it to the public, be it on radio, television or in print.

Journalism covers a vast spectrum of jobs. From a trainee reporter on a local newspaper, to the editor of a glossy monthly magazine, from a young writer on a sports magazine to a presenter on BBC's *Six O'Clock News*, all are journalists.

The following are some prominent journalists: Trevor McDonald, presenter of *News At Ten*; Andrew Neil, newspaper columnist and television presenter; Alistair Campbell, press officer for Tony Blair, the Prime Minister; Suzanne Moore, *Independent* columnist; Gary Bushell, writer for *The Sun*; Caitlin Moran, *Times* feature writer and columnist.

Seven areas of journalism

In Britain, journalists work for **newspapers, magazines, radio, television** and **news agencies**. Any journalist working for one of these five media will need similar skills. They can also work in **public relations** and **book publishing**, where jobs are very different from those in the rest of the media.

Newspapers can be national or provincial, daily, weekly and even bi-weekly. Their circulation varies from a few thousand to almost five million. Two examples: the *News of The World* sells just under five million copies each Sunday; the Peterborough *Evening Telegraph* sells about 35,000 copies a day. Most are paid for, but some local newspapers are free.

Magazines can be weekly, monthly or quarterly, and range from tiny to mass-circulation. They cover an enormous range of subjects and their circulations are spread over just as wide a scale. A few examples: *Smash Hits*, aimed at teenagers, sells more than 300,000 copies a week; the up-market title *Tatler* sells around 85,000 copies a month; the *Spectator*, which runs mostly features on current affairs, sells more than 50,000 a week.

Many journalists work in **television** and **radio**, from the BBC's local stations to ITN. They work on programmes like the BBC's *Breakfast News* or the *Today* programme on Radio 4. Others also make a good living as **freelances** – that is, they are self-employed and sell specific articles, ideas or scripts to radio or television programmes.

There are also **news agencies**. Some are international, such as Reuters, some national, like the Press Association, and many more which are local to one town, city or area, some staffed by a single journalist.

What is journalism?

The heart of the journalist's job is to find information and pass it on to a wider audience. Some journalists **gather** news – reporters, feature writers or specialist correspondents. And some **process** it – sub-editors, news editors, editors.

The majority of journalists start out as **reporters**. A reporter can be asked to cover almost any event or write on an infinite variety of subjects.

- *National newspapers* report not only the day's domestic news but also sport, the arts, foreign news, politics, royal and social events, fashion, food, women's interest subjects, travel, property, do-it-yourself, motoring and gardening.

- *Local papers* report news, community affairs and local events – even down to the results of agricultural shows.

- There are around 7,500 *periodicals* published in this country, covering an enormous, and growing, range of subjects from angling, antiques and art, to fashion, food and football. As well as the magazines we see on the news-stands, there are trade and technical titles which are usually sold, by subscription, to a particular group of professional people or members of an organisation.

A journalist might report for any of the above. He or she might also become an **editor**, of a publication or a television or radio programme, or of a section within a publication.

Journalists with some **experience** can move away from reporting into many other areas – making documentaries for television, presenting a radio news programme, editing a house magazine for a large company, writing a regular column for a particular publication, advising a politician, or setting up his or her own news agency.

They can also become press or public relations officers for companies, individuals or organisations, and some are employed in book publishing.

GETTING STARTED

'The message is clear; if you are looking for an entrée into journalism, think laterally, and cast your net wide.'
Maggie Brown, Media Editor (*The Independent*)

'Q: What single quality do you feel has got you this far? A: One thing that counts in my favour is my enthusiasm.'
Sybil Ruscoe, presenter for Radio 5 Live (*Today*)

The choice of jobs in journalism is enormous, and the competition for them is intense. Journalists can be **staff** or **freelance** but almost all begin in salaried jobs to gain the necessary experience.

How do you get into the profession?
You can do one of two things: either get your own training before applying for jobs, or apply to one of the media which offers on-the-job training.

- Journalism **courses** at colleges and universities are proliferating and there is a growing trend towards employing graduates.

- However, it is still possible for a school-leaver with A-levels to find a job as a **trainee reporter**.

- In **newspapers,** training leading to a National Certificate or an NVQ is compulsory.

- Most **magazines** also offer training, although it is not compulsory.

- In **television**, there are openings for only a very few graduate trainees. **Radio** has a small number of openings. BBC and ITN take on only a handful of inexperienced recruits each year. Other than these, radio and television recruit experienced journalists only.

- **Public relations** organisations take on some graduate trainees.

- In **books,** training is available but not compulsory.

Is it best to get training, and then hunt for a job? Or try to find a job where training will be provided?
There is no simple answer, unfortunately. Training – even a degree in journalism – does not guarantee you a job.

In 1991, three higher education colleges launched the first degrees in journalism in Britain. When their graduates emerged into the real world in the summer of 1994, their experiences varied considerably. A survey by *The Journalist*, the magazine of the National Union of Journalists, found that by January 1995:

- One of 30 graduates from City University had a definite job. (Not all had left; some were on a four-year course.)

- 75 per cent of 32 graduates of the London College of Printing had jobs.

- 40 per cent of 34 graduates from the University of Central Lancashire had jobs.

Competition for trainee posts in all media is fierce. The BBC advises potential recruits: 'All routes are highly competitive and only the best succeed. If you are a young person considering journalism as a career, don't just set your sights on the BBC. Training opportunities attract a large response. Keep other options open.' (*The Way In: Job Opportunities*, 1992.)

Changes in recruitment

Traditionally, journalists were recruited as school-leavers and trained on the job.

This was changing fast in the mid-1990s, as a survey for the Guild of Editors showed. The report, in February 1995, concluded that 'entry into journalism is in danger of being dominated by middle-class graduates, often from the mushrooming media courses.'

But some editors in the provinces disagreed, arguing that provincial journalism was losing touch with its readers. Barry Williams, then editor of the *Nottingham Evening Post*, began recruiting local trainees and basing them on housing estates. Alan Jones, editorial director of *Southern Newspapers*, changed the company's recruitment guidelines so that editors could take on promising school-leavers once again.

How can I find the best route in?

As you can see, there is a complex network of ways into journalism. To sum up:

- School-leavers can apply to newspapers, magazines and radio for their various trainee posts. They can also apply for journalism or media courses at colleges and universities.

- Graduates can also apply to newspapers, magazines, radio, television and news agencies for traineeships.

- Alternatively, anyone can set up as a freelance, although the inexperienced will find it very hard work.

What experience is useful?

When you apply for a place on a course, a post as a trainee, or even your first job, your chances will be much better if you have some experience of journalism. How do you get it? The obvious place is a school or university magazine or newspaper where you can begin writing and sub-editing (cutting copy, writing headlines, checking accuracy). You could also:

- Write letters for publication in newspapers and magazines.

- Contribute to newsletters produced by local organisations.

- Submit some short features to various publications. If you go on holiday, write a travel article and offer it to local or national newspapers.

- Learn to type and, if you want to go into print journalism, begin learning shorthand.

- If you are aiming to be a broadcaster, try to get a spell of work experience on local radio or television stations.

- Get involved in whatever would illustrate your commitment to your chosen profession; for example, if your heart is set on becoming a political correspondent, offer to work in the local MP's constituency office or for a local political party. If you are ambitious to become a radio reporter, offer to work for nothing at your local radio station in your holidays.

- Read as wide a variety of newspapers as possible; watch television and listen to radio news bulletins and make sure you are fully informed about current affairs.

- Look out for any opportunity to get into print, on the air or on videotape. Keep a cuttings book or diary of all your pre-work experience.

The first days at work
Almost all journalists start off by learning similar basic skills. They are taught to:

- **Report** current events. They learn how to write news reports, scripts or features.

- **Research** the background to a story, using reference books and cuttings.

- **Interview** people, from the man in the street to an official spokesman.

- **Take notes or use tape/video**: print journalists will learn shorthand, broadcast journalists how to operate radio or television equipment.

Journalists also need to develop an understanding of:

- **The law**: how it affects court reporting, and how someone could be libelled.

- **Public affairs**: how national and local government work.

- **Ethics**: the codes of conduct governing journalists' behaviour and the privacy of the public.

- **What makes news**: journalists must learn quickly what makes a story.

Building a career

Once a journalist is a competent news reporter, he or she may move on. The qualified journalist will be able to choose whether to concentrate on one particular subject or to continue reporting general news.

Some become **specialists**, reporting and commenting on one subject in great detail. An example is the theatre critic. Another is the fashion editor.

Other journalists may prefer to remain as **general news reporters** or **feature writers**. They would cover a much wider range of subjects and have less detailed knowledge of any one.

News and features

There is a difference between a news reporter and a feature writer although both write about or broadcast on current events. The **reporter** will cover an event as it happens, or as soon as possible afterwards. His job is to interview those involved and compile a report of the facts. His report will be impartial and balanced.

The **feature writer** may compose an article or programme on the same event. It will be longer than the news story and will look at the implications or analyse what happened and why. The feature may contain opinion or ask questions.

The two roles exist because, historically, newspapers have always divided up their pages into 'news' and 'features'. The aim is to give the reader a balance between 'hard' and 'soft' writing and between reportage and analysis/comment.

The division also exists in **broadcasting**. News is transmitted to the public in **bulletins** – crisp, concise headlines and brief, factual reports with short interviews. Features, investigations and documentaries come under the heading **current affairs**, and are typically longer and more analytical.

Flexibility

Once qualified, journalists commonly switch between different media. Print-trained reporters and sub-editors often move into radio or television; journalists switch from newspapers to magazines and vice versa; print and broadcast journalists become public relations officers or authors.

Staff writers may go freelance, and freelances may take up staff jobs. Many people in the profession have a variety of employment – writing and broadcasting, journalism and books, broadcasting and teaching. It is a flexible and unrestricted profession with a wealth of opportunities which you can tailor to your own needs.

BASIC SKILLS

'Comment is free but facts are sacred.'
C. P. Scott, editor, *Manchester Guardian* (1926)

'It is not the world that has got so much worse, but the news coverage that has got so much better.'
G. K. Chesterton

Whichever of the many diverse jobs in journalism you set out to do, you will need to learn the skills mentioned earlier.

Getting the facts

A journalist discovers what he or she thinks would make a good story. But before it can be published or broadcast, it must be proved to be accurate. All the relevant facts must be discovered and checked. How?

To find out the **background**, a journalist will look at relevant published or broadcast material. This could be cuttings, back copies of newspapers or magazines, reference books, on-line library data, tapes or videotapes.

Once he or she knows the history of whatever is being investigated, the reporting begins. Reporting is finding new information, either by observation or through interviews.

- *Observation* can be anything from going to a council meeting to hear a debate, to spending a day with a junior doctor at a hospital to report on doctors' hours.

- *Interviewing* can range from a few snatched moments in the street to a half-hour on the telephone or an in-depth talk over lunch. It can be pre-arranged, or off the cuff.

  Interviewing is skill which takes practice. The journalist has to prise out the information he or she wants, not what his interviewee wants to tell him. You may have to sift through a lot of useless information to identify the facts you can use.

Some tips on reporting:

- Always take notes about what you see. You will never remember everything.

- Write down or tape the answers of everyone you interview, at the time.

- Check the spelling of names and places. Do not assume Smith is spelt that way – it could be Smyth.

- Think about the questions you want to ask before an interview.

- Make a list.

- Know what to expect. If you have been sent to interview a pop personality, research him first.

- Make frequent check calls to your newsroom. They may have information or new instructions for you.

- Make using your equipment second nature. If you are struggling to keep up in shorthand, or fiddling with a tape recorder, you may miss an important quote.

- Don't give up. If a door is slammed in your face, try the next one.

You will want your story to answer five basic questions: **who**?

what? where? why? and **when?** Keeping digging until you have the answers!

Turning the facts into a story

When you have assembled your information, it is time to put it together for publication or broadcast.

You will need to know how many words you are required to write, or how much air time you have been allocated. Tailor your report accordingly.

News reports or scripts must follow certain rules. They must be:

- *Accurate* – you must be sure of your facts.

- *Legal* – you must not print or broadcast information prohibited by the law, such as the identity of a rape victim.

- *Fair and balanced* – they must reflect both sides of a story. For example, if your report criticises a local council, that council must be allowed room for a response.

- *Objective* – news reports do not normally contain opinion or comment.

- *Clear, concise and to the point* – news reports are not intended to be creatively written, but to present information in a simple and logical way. They can include reported speech or direct quotes but should be free of jargon and cliché.

These guidelines apply to newspapers, radio and television.

More than a story: features and current affairs

Writing features for magazines or newspapers, or scripting current affairs programmes for radio or television, is slightly different. You will still need to be accurate, legal, fair and balanced, and express yourself clearly and concisely. But features or documentaries usually allow for **analysis** and **comment** as well.

If you are writing a feature, you will be able to do more than report the facts. You will be able to present an argument and draw a conclusion.

Your newspaper may ask you to write from a particular point of view. For example, you could be asked to do a piece on a plan for redevelopment in the town centre but, unlike in a news story, arguing against it.

The same is true of current affairs programmes. The facts will form the backbone of your tape or film, but you will be able to present it as an argument or to analyse your subject in more depth. For example, you may be preparing a short film on the facilities at local hospitals. As the presenter, you may be able to put forward the argument that the hospitals cannot cope with a growing population. To keep the film fair and balanced, you would include someone – a doctor or health service official – who disagrees.

THE JOURNALIST'S LIFESTYLE

'News is what someone wants to stop you printing. All the rest is advertisements.'

William Randolph Hearst, American newspaper proprietor

'The hours are quite punishing with some Sundays and evenings going by the board. This is always the problem for women.'

Georgina Henry, deputy editor, *The Guardian*

- Journalists may find themselves working in or out of the office, and probably a mixture of both. Those working for national media may be based anywhere in Britain, or even abroad.

- They may have to work both days and nights at times, on a rota basis.

- If a story they have been working on develops on a day off, they may be called in. Similarly, if a big story breaks, they may be needed.

- If they are on holiday, and a story breaks in that location, their editor will almost certainly ask for their help.

- They may have to fit their holiday plans around their work. For example, a political editor is unlikely to take holidays during the party conference season.

- They may have to travel at short notice. They often have to work a much longer day than expected, say, if they are covering a meeting which overruns.

- Much of the journalist's work can also be distressing. He or she may have to interview someone who has been recently bereaved.

- They may have to ask questions of someone who has just survived a disaster, such as the sinking of a ferry. They also have to report first-hand descriptions of major tragedies, such as earthquakes or air crashes.

- Many jobs are dangerous. A journalist working abroad may find himself or herself in an area where a virulent disease is taking hold. It is often necessary to venture into or near a war zone. Journalists reporting on a demonstration may find themselves in the middle of a riot.

- Getting the news is never easy. Officials will try to stop you finding out what you want to know. Celebrities can slam the door in your face or refuse to answer the telephone. Club-owners may throw you out. The police might say: 'Sorry, you can't come in here.'

As the above makes clear, anyone contemplating journalism as a career needs to be aware that it is not an easy life.

CASE STUDIES

The editor
Magnus Linklater was Editor of *The Scotsman* from 1988 to 1994. He is now a *Times* writer.

His career began on the *Daily Express* in 1964. He moved to the *Evening Standard* in London where he became editor of the Londoner's Diary. In 1969 he joined the *Sunday Times* where he worked for fourteen years, including editing the colour magazine. In 1983 he joined *The Observer* and three years later launched the *London Daily News*. He has written several books.

How I began in journalism
I came down from Cambridge with a modest degree in modern languages and no idea about a career. I was introduced to the Features Editor of the *Daily Express* who invited me in to meet the Editor. Result: a job as a junior reporter in the Manchester office. Qualifications: nil.

What attracted me to the profession?
It seemed a reasonable way of making a living until I found a proper job. Gradually it became addictive.

My working day
As editor of *The Scotsman*, I arrived at approximately 10am, read the papers, took calls and handled problems. At 11am we had our morning conference. Then there were meetings and a possible lunch appointment or interview. At 3.45pm was our second conference, followed by the leader conference. At about 5.30pm I would go and sit on the backbench to choose stories and pictures for the news pages. Then I would write and edit the leaders. I'd go home at about 9.30pm and at 11pm the first edition would be delivered. Then I'd call the news desk and the backbench for changes and corrections.

My finest piece of work
Investigating a kidnapping case in Sardinia in 1980.

One piece of advice
Never let a story go. There's always an angle to be got that your rivals may not have found.

The radio reporter
Susanna Bateman is a senior reporter with GWR FM Radio News at Swindon, Wiltshire. She attended Manchester University from 1990 to 1993 and gained a BA Joint Honours in Media Studies with Business Management and Information Technology (first class). She joined GWR in 1993.

How I began in journalism
I did a City and Guilds radio and journalism course alongside A-levels before going to do a university degree. During the second year of my degree I did a nine-week industrial placement at GWR FM in the newsroom, which led to freelance work after I graduated. I was then taken on the staff and worked my way up from a trainee to a senior reporter.

What attracted me to the profession?
Unpredictability. Tight deadlines. A fresh challenge daily.

My working day
Early reading: Arrive at work at 5am. Do a full round of check calls and compile, edit and read news bulletins every hour (and half hour at breakfast) until 1pm. Finish around 2.30pm.

Late reading: Work from around 10am. Do a couple of hours reporting, generating news for the afternoon. After midday the early reader hands the desk over to me and I compile, edit and read the news until 6pm. After that I finish off loose ends, return phone calls and tidy the desk for the morning.

My finest piece of work
An outside broadcast from RAF Lyneham in August 1994 when I did the 7am news bulletin live from the radio car. Interviews and material I'd sent back to the newsroom earlier had been edited and were 'driven' from the studio while I presented the bulletin from Lyneham. The story was that all British troops flying to Rwanda were taking off from the Wiltshire base.

One piece of advice
Arrange work placements with as many journalistic outlets as you can, i.e. newspapers, radio, TV, freelance agencies, to gain experience and initiate contacts. It's all part of 'getting your foot in the door.'

The managing editor
Patrick Pilton is Group Managing Editor of Mirror Group Newspapers. He started as a trainee reporter on the *Pontypridd Observer*. He has worked for many publications including the *Western Mail and Echo*, the *Evening Post* (Reading), the *Daily Mirror*, *The Sun*, the *Daily Express* and *Today*. He edited the *Sunday Sun* (Newcastle) and the *South Wales Echo* (Cardiff).

How I began in journalism
A lucky break. I switched to reading the *Daily Telegraph* and on the second day of buying it there was an advertisement for 'adult entrants' into journalism on a South Wales weekly. Hundreds applied and two of us, amazingly with no experience, were chosen on trial at £8 a week. We were both kept on. Thirty years later the editor's wife revealed to me that I was not even on the shortlist for interview. She liked my letter and slipped it in unbeknown to the

boss. I will for ever be grateful.

What attracted me to the profession

The excitement and glamour; wanting to write. I was so infatuated with newspapers that in my teens I would walk along Fleet Street every Sunday just to feel part of it. Nothing has changed.

My working day

It is so eclectic a job that no two days are ever the same. In any one day I might find myself interviewing and recruiting young journalists; battling with a budget that is £20 million overspent; briefing editors; discussing strategy with the Managing Director or Chief Executive; negotiating contracts; finding missing mice for the Apple Mac terminals; and dealing with a shortage of tampons in the ladies' loo.

My finest piece of work

I was fortunate to be chief sub on the day of the moon landing, and night editor on the nights that the Falklands and Gulf wars began. And the night Elvis Presley died. But 'memorable' is probably a more appropriate description than 'finest'. Cutting a major *Daily Mirror* feature writer's piece by half and earning his thanks for my efforts probably gave me most satisfaction. Sub-editing is a wonderful, and now sadly devalued, art.

One piece of advice

Always check and double check your facts. Never doctor them to embellish a story or to fit a preconceived idea of what you, or your editor, wants it to be.

The news editor

Gordon Ducker is associate news editor of the *Daily Express*. He started on a weekly newspaper, the *Sevenoaks News*, in Kent. He has worked on many national and local newspapers, including *The Star* in Sheffield, the *Sevenoaks Chronicle* and the *Sunday Express*. His previous jobs include news reporter, crime reporter, showbusiness reporter, columnist, feature writer and news editor.

How I began in journalism

When an editor visited my school careers evening, his advice was: 'Never mind A-levels, the way to learn this job is out on the street doing it.' I took it to heart. A round of letter writing to all weekly newspapers within a 30-mile radius of my home produced few replies. I called at the offices of my two local papers, explained that I wanted to be a journalist and asked to see the editor. Both visits produced interviews and, four days after leaving school, I became a junior reporter.

What attracted me to the profession?
The chance to combine writing with getting out and about, meeting a wide range of people and being at or near the centre of important events. At 16, I believed I could 'tell it like it is' – inform the public, expose injustices, right wrongs.

My working day
- Hectic, fraught, exciting, the working day begins the night before. Check call to night news editor for a rundown on news events and what stories the opposition are carrying. Discuss deploying reporters.

- At 6am news gathering and filtering process begins. Radio and TV news bulletins switched on.

- Arrive at office at 7.30am; check night log, futures list – schedule of that day's events – and Press Association news schedule. Scan late editions of other national newspapers.

- District reporters and specialist writers start ringing in.

- A constant flow of information from news desk staff is directed at the news editor. His job is to assess it all, decide what stories are right for his newspaper, which reporter should cover which story, come up with exclusives and original ideas for angles on stories.

- First three hours are hectic as schedule for 10.30am conference, chaired by the editor, is prepared.

- At about 12.30pm an early paging conference with the editor or his deputy will begin to decide where stories and pictures will be used in the paper. Brief lunch. The flow of copy into the computer has become a flood.

- By 4.30pm conference, news pages are taking shape. As well as keeping a watch for new stories, the news editor is checking copy that has come in from staff reporters.

- At around 7.30pm the last of the first edition stories has left the news desk. The news editor's day hasn't quite finished – he has to think about tomorrow.

My finest piece of work

No journalist is ever happy when he looks back at something he has written. That caveat apart, the work that gave me the greatest satisfaction was my year as a member of the five-man 'On Our Conscience' team set up by the editor of the *Sheffield Star*. I was one of the reporters who found an elderly woman on New Year's Day – covered in a ragged blanket in a sparsely furnished, filthy, freezing council tenement. She was 80, had been ill for years, yet no one had been near her for weeks. Her story became the springboard for our campaign.

By the end of the year more than 1,300 cases had been investigated; slum landlords, council departments, welfare services, the then DHSS and public service companies were among those taken to task in stories and features.

A dossier was compiled and led to a reorganisation of the way social services operated. And the year's work won the IPC Campaigning Journalist of the Year Award.

One piece of advice

Before you've got your first job – never give in. If you want to become a journalist enough, you will.

Once you're in – always remember the readers are the most important people so write your stories or headlines for them. And guard against ever thinking you are more important than they are.

The provincial newspaper editor

Rachael Campey became editor of Exeter's *Express & Echo* in March 1991. Before that, she was deputy editor of the *Northern Echo*, a regional morning paper in the north-east. Prior to this, she worked at the *Coventry Evening Telegraph*. She started as a reporter on a weekly paper – the *Solihull News*.

Rachael is a graduate of Liverpool University with a BA Honours in History. She also worked on the graduate management scheme in the National Health Service. One of her interests is walking.

How I began in journalism

As a trainee reporter on the *Solihull News*. It was not my first job. After graduating, I went into NHS management, on the graduate training scheme, and it was really then that my interest in journalism began. I worked in London and Kent for a year doing different jobs, including porter and nursing auxiliary. I wrote an article about the training. It was published and I decided to go into journalism. I wrote to every paper in the *Willing's Guide* and got an interview at West Midlands Press (the *Solihull News*) and never looked back.

I also believe my degree in history and curiosity about people helped.

What attracted me to the profession?

People. Their stories. I met a wide variety of people during my two NHS years and coming straight after university it gave me street-wise experience which proved invaluable when I entered journalism.

I also admired other journalists with the ability to convey pictures in words – James Cameron, Alistair Cooke. The unpretentious, enlightening style of journalism certainly helped draw me to the profession.

A brief description of my working day

- Conference at 7.30 each morning.
- Assessing stories and legal checks.
- Writing editorial comment.
- Reviewing page one for each of six editions (daily).
- Five ten-minute radio bulletins each day – this is an on-air update which I give to local radio on news breaking in the *Express & Echo* that day.
- Answering mail.
- Giving talks/presentations – a great deal of PR and community work – a fair amount in the evenings.
- Planning ahead with other department heads – newspaper sales/promotions/advertising/production. Daily meetings.
- I am also on the board of directors of the *Express & Echo* PLC.
- Regular board meetings.
- Handling my own editorial budget.

My finest piece of work

Professionally, being an editor and doing all of the above.

As a journalist, two fine areas of work:

1. Handling the coverage of the Cleveland child abuse crisis as news editor of the *Northern Echo*.

2. Masterminding the campaign to win compensation for haemophiliacs who had contracted the AIDS virus. We won. We were also runners up in the British Press Awards.

Advice for aspiring journalists
*   Know the audience you are writing for.
*   Don't assume anything.
*   Ask the questions readers would ask – and want to know the answers to.
*   Be very curious.
*   Think stories.
*   Learn to talk to/with people. Be at ease and put others at ease.
*   Listen.
*   Always be accurate.
*   Have very good spelling and don't skimp on grammar – or the apostrophe.

2

Which Job is for You?

'The only qualities essential for real success in journalism are ratlike cunning, a plausible manner and a little literary ability.'
Nicholas Tomalin, journalist

'First you need to have certain in-built qualities; strong determination to be a journalist, an insatiable thirst for knowledge, a very keen interest in news and current events and the ability to write well.'
A Future In Broadcast Journalism, National Council for the Training of Broadcast Journalists

A JOB TO SUIT YOU

There are as many different kinds of job in journalism as there are publications. And journalism is one of those careers in which you can indulge your own interests.

If clothes are your passion, you could enter fashion journalism. If you are interested in cinema, there is the opportunity for reviewing films. If you love cricket, then perhaps you could be a sports correspondent. You may decide you want to move from news-gathering to news processing, becoming a sub-editor, section editor or editor of a publication. But competition for such specialist jobs is fierce. You will need to be both very sure of what you want to do and single-minded about working towards it.

Most journalists start off by news reporting; opportunities then open up as their careers progress.

Print or broadcast?

You will need to decide which is your chosen form of communication before applying for jobs or training. Of course, you can apply to more than one section of the media.

If you enjoy writing and have a good command of grammar and spelling, newspapers and magazines will be your best bet. If you feel at home with a tape recorder, radio may be your choice. Perhaps you have been involved in video or film-making, and so choose television.

Whichever medium you aim for, you will find that the basics of journalism are the same. News reporters will gather information in a similar way, whether it is for the local weekly newspaper, national television or a large radio station. It is simply how you present your information to your audience that is different.

Changing jobs

It is possible, once you are a qualified journalist, to switch from one medium to another. Polly Toynbee, now a senior journalist on *The Independent*, was previously with BBC Television. Liz Forgan has been managing director of BBC Network Radio, director of programmes at Channel 4 and Women's Editor of *The Guardian*. Neil Duncanson, managing director of Chrysalis Sport which makes programmes for national television, began as a trainee reporter on the *Newham Recorder*.

Some journalists combine working for two or more different media. There are many television presenters who also write columns for magazines and newspapers, such as Kirsty Young, Channel 5 presenter and *Daily Express* columnist. Within the BBC, it is common for journalists to work for both radio and television.

There is also the option of photo-journalism. The photo-journalist, usually a freelance, will put together a package of words and photographs (or, increasingly, colour transparencies) which she or he will sell to a magazine or newspaper. Travel and showbusiness celebrities make ideal subjects for photo-journalism.

Variety and flexibility

Journalists have great flexibility in how they work. For instance, if you decide to aim for television you could find yourself working for a large organisation, such as Independent Television News, where you are backed up by a cameraman and sound and lighting staff. Or you could become one of a new breed of videojournalists, employed by cable operators, where you are a one-person operation, interviewing while carrying your camcorder on your shoulder.

In radio, you may end up on the road, reporting from the scene, you may be conducting interviews in a studio or you could become a programme editor.

On a magazine, where staff numbers tend to be smaller than in the other sections of the media, you could end up doing several jobs – writing a feature on Monday and Tuesday, helping to edit copy on a

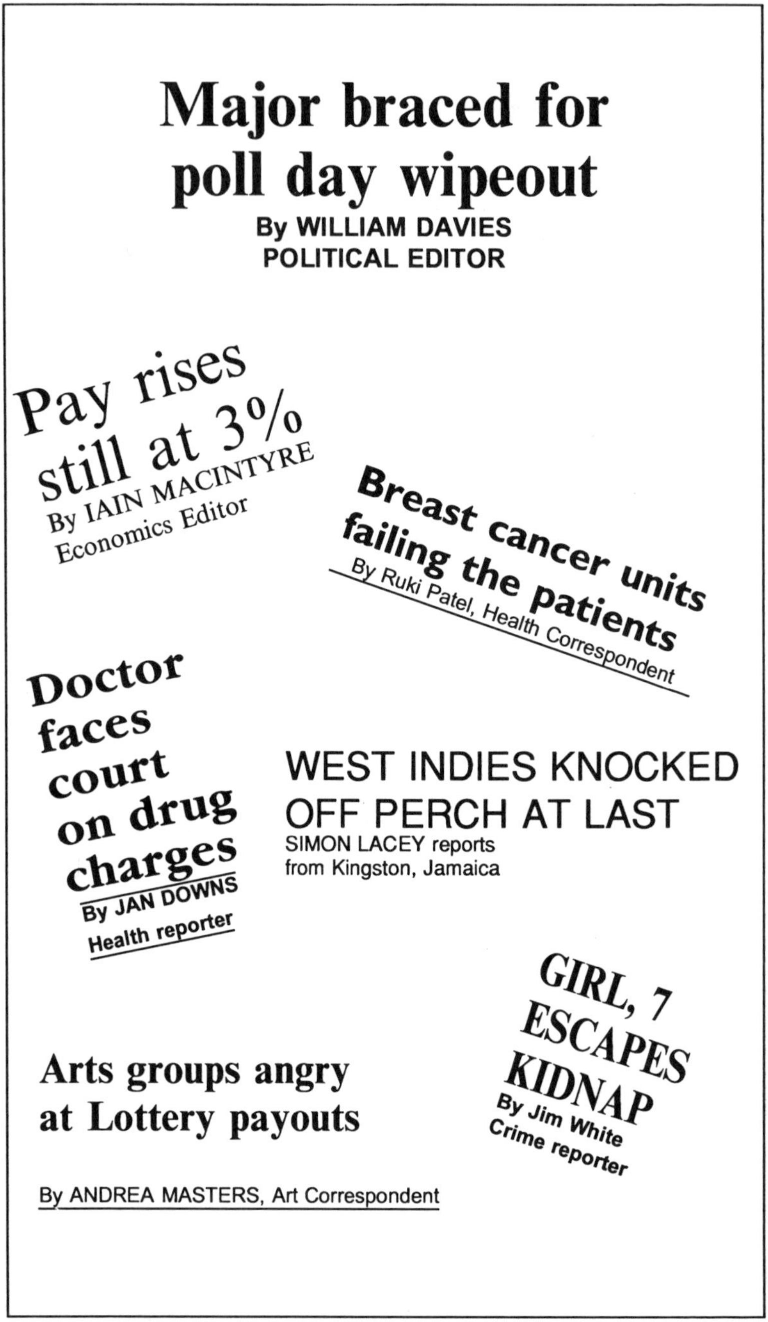

Major braced for poll day wipeout

By WILLIAM DAVIES
POLITICAL EDITOR

Pay rises still at 3%

By IAIN MACINTYRE
Economics Editor

Breast cancer units failing the patients

By Ruki Patel, Health Correspondent

Doctor faces court on drug charges

By JAN DOWNS
Health reporter

WEST INDIES KNOCKED OFF PERCH AT LAST

SIMON LACEY reports
from Kingston, Jamaica

GIRL, 7 ESCAPES KIDNAP

By Jim White
Crime reporter

Arts groups angry at Lottery payouts

By ANDREA MASTERS, Art Correspondent

Fig. 1. Specialists and their bylines.

34

Wednesday and Thursday, sifting through readers' letters on Friday morning and interviewing a celebrity in the afternoon. On the smaller, specialist magazines it is quite common to do both writing and editing. On mass-circulation titles, the crossover is less.

WHAT ARE THE JOBS ON OFFER?

While it would be impossible to list every media post, here is a selection of some of the jobs you might end up in. (See Figure 1.)

Reporter, evening newspaper

This is where many journalists begin. As a trainee reporter, you work in the office and outside. You might accompany a senior reporter to learn about interviewing and investigating, court and council reporting. You would also work in the office making 'check calls' – to the emergency services such as police, ambulance and fire brigade, to find out what news events are happening.

You would cover a wide range of stories – social and community issues, crime, human interest stories and local activities of all kinds including sport.

Here are some of the stories a junior reporter could expect to be sent on:

- Reporting on a campaign by residents of a particular street to get a pedestrian crossing installed.

- Writing a feature piece on the appeal of an old-fashioned funfair which is currently visiting town.

- Reporting on a minor league football match.

- Interviewing a teenager from a local school who saved the life of a fellow pupil on a recent canoeing trip.

- Carrying out street interviews of local residents to their reaction to the news that a major foreign car manufacturer is to build a factory in the town.

- Covering the story of a local child who has disappeared, including press conferences held by police, an interview with the child's parents and a reconstruction of her last known movements.

- Reporting from the set of a new film being made in nearby countryside.

- Attending the press launch of a new, local cheese – and finding out what people think of it.

- Working as one of a team of three reporters sent to cover a major road accident on a nearby motorway. Taking eyewitness accounts from survivors and emergency services at the scene, speaking to families of those involved and attending press conferences at the police station and the local hospital. The story would need constant updating for later editions, as the number of dead and injured became clear and as more facts emerged.

- Attending local council meetings. Reporting debates on planning, education, transport and housing.

- Reporting magistrates' court cases including burglaries, thefts and fraud, driving offences and charges of violent behaviour.

- Working with a senior reporter who is covering the closure of a local hospital. This is a long-running story and could include reporting on a campaign by health workers and residents to keep it open, a visit by the Health Minister to the hospital, interviewing a local doctor who says the building is unsuitable and should be closed, and attending a public meeting at which health officials make their case for closure.

- Reviewing a pop concert at the town theatre and trying to get an interview with the well-known performer afterwards.

Junior reporter jobs on local newspapers are open to those entering journalism and are the most popular way into the profession.

Arts correspondent, network radio

Journalists knowledgeable about the arts can work in almost any branch of the media. As an example, let's look at the arts correspondent of a national radio station.

This is her brief: to contribute stories and features on both the visual arts – painting, sculpture and 'installation art' exhibitions – and the performing arts – including theatre, dance and opera.

Her day-to-day work is very varied. She might be reporting on a new exhibition of paintings, a new play, film or musical. She will also carry out interviews with people from the arts world who are in the news – a famous sculptor, a dancer, or even an ex-prisoner turned painter.

Here are some of the stories she has covered in her first few months:

- She wrote and broadcast a report about a painting stolen from a stately home. A news reporter compiled a report about the actual theft. The arts correspondent's job was to provide a complementary piece giving the background information on the painting – a profile of the artist, the painting's value, its provenance (previous owners and the locations at which it was held).

- She has interviewed a young sculptor awarded a major arts prize.

- She has scripted and presented a half-hour programme on a highly successful impresario with three musicals running in London's West End.

- She has scripted and presented a feature piece about the behind-the-scenes life of a regional ballet company, using interviews and actuality (recordings of what is actually happening, such as a rehearsal).

The radio station runs a weekly arts programme for which she is responsible. It is designed to inform listeners about current and forthcoming events from exhibitions to musicals. She finds stories, does both live and recorded interviews and compiles a 'what's on' bulletin which she reads on air.

Journalists seeking this job would need to be qualified and probably have a degree in an arts-related subject.

Editor, football magazine

This journalist leads a small team producing a weekly magazine dedicated to covering our national sport. He edits the magazine which involves deciding the content, overseeing the layout, representing the magazine at various events – such as an awards ceremony – and also writing his own column. And when he is not doing all of that, he covers some matches.

His staff is made up of four full-time writers, with several others paid a retainer to cover matches when needed, a chief sub-editor, two sub-editors, a designer and administrative staff. He reports directly to the magazine's publisher.

A typical day might be like this:

- Morning editorial conference with staff to decide the content of the next issue.

- Briefing writers, both in the office and by telephone.

- A meeting with the advertising department or the marketing department to discuss pagination (the size) of the next issue and to talk about future strategy.

- Lunch with the chairman of a leading club, during which he interviews him for a profile he intends to write.

- Watching a game in the evening, which he will write up later.

- He also writes a 'gossip' column for each issue.

What does it take to become editor of a small, specialist magazine, be it about football or any other subject? Obviously, great enthusiasm for that subject, a good knowledge of it, the ability to get to know the people involved and a solid grounding in journalism.

This job combines all the skills of reporting, feature writing and interviewing with many others. Such an editor would need an eye for design, the ability to manage and motivate staff, a knowledge of marketing a magazine and controlling budgets, familiarity with magazine printing processes and even some public speaking experience.

He or she would need to be a good organiser, capable of working alone and of carrying a heavy responsibility.

Literary editor, Sunday newspaper

Her job: choosing new books to be reviewed, commissioning reviews of some of them and writing reviews of others herself. She also contributes to the news pages with stories about authors, the books business and major figures in that industry. She spends much time out of the office, talking to people involved in the literary world at book launches and awards ceremonies.

An example of one of her most recent stories might be this: a highly successful author has sacked his agent and is looking for a new one, with the proviso that the replacement must be able to get him a £500,000 advance for his next novel.

She reports from literary awards ceremonies, such as the Booker Prize, and interviews the winning author. A takeover of a publishing company, a previously unknown author whose first novel had made it into the top ten best-sellers and the obituary of a well-known writer would all be handled by the books editor.

Consumer affairs correspondent, regional television

Our correspondent works for a television station covering a large area in the north of England. He has a wide brief – to report on anything that affects ordinary consumers, from a supermarket price war to changes in the laws governing the selling of alcohol on Sundays.

He may have to interview the chairman of one of the privatised utilities, such as British Gas, after a price rise, report on the first day of the January sales or produce a short feature about the best bargain holiday destinations.

Here are some of the recent programmes our consumer correspondent has been involved in:

- A series broadcast in four parts during the early evening news programme. The subject: how out-of-town supermarkets are destroying high streets in small towns throughout the area. He spoke to shopkeepers in such towns, to supermarket managers and press officers, to shoppers and to traders' organisations. He did some live interviews, reporting to camera, and wrote and read scripts to sections of 'actuality'. Each lasted only two minutes, but a considerable amount of reporting and editing has gone into them.

- He has reported live from a demonstration by animal rights activists against the export of live calves from a local port.

- He has scripted a news report on a fall in charges by British Telecom.

- He has carried out a studio interview with the managing director of a small local company which has won a contract to supply the royal household with hand-made chocolates.

- He has carried out street interviews with local residents to get their reaction to the closure of several post offices.

Newspapers, magazines and radio stations also employ consumer correspondents. A fully trained news reporter could move into this job. He or she would not need any specialist knowledge.

District reporter, weekly newspaper

This reporter works for a large weekly newspaper group in the south west of England. The paper has six editions, circulating in a sizeable city and the smaller towns around.

This district reporter is one of four based in outlying towns. He is relatively inexperienced, yet carries a great deal of responsibility for finding and covering stories in his own area. He covers routine events on his own patch, such as town council meetings and sessions at the magistrates' court. He makes police calls and checks with the other emergency services.

He has also built up a list of contacts – people whom he can call upon for information or who may tip him off about stories. Among them are the town mayor, headmasters of several schools, a local police inspector, publicans, shopkeepers, people involved with action groups of all kinds and other journalists covering the area.

He has a small office in the town which he shares with an advertisement representative and a secretary. He is provided with a company car, because most of his stories require him to travel around the area.

What does he write about? Community affairs and local matters of all kinds, human interest stories, agriculture (as this is a rural area), and anything else that happens on his patch. At the moment, he is covering the progress of controversial plans to build a town bypass. It is possible there will be a public inquiry into the plans, and if so he will report that along with journalists from national media.

For the feature pages of his newspaper, he has written a series about village life in the 1990s. That involved interviewing people of all ages and from all walks of life in several surrounding villages. He talked to them about transport problems, a shortage of housing for rent, falling property prices, closure of village schools, high prices in small grocery shops, and why they would or would not move back to a town.

The job of district reporter is open to all journalists, including trainees, providing they have mastered the skills of research and writing, have a good knowledge of newspaper law and are well organised and capable of working alone.

Financial writer, London

The financial reporter in our example works for London's only evening newspaper, which has several pages of City news each day. Her job is to find and write stories on everything to do with the City and the financial world – share movements, interest rates, what companies are doing and their financial results.

She will need to develop good contacts within banks, building societies and the stock market. She might be writing about a rise in interest rates one day, a plunge in a company's profits the next, a building society merger the day after.

One of our city reporter's routine tasks is to do an interview each week with someone involved in the financial world. It could be a banker or the chief executive of a private company or public corporation, a share dealer or a financial analyst. She will write about 800 words on each one and her report will be accompanied by a photograph.

What sort of questions will she ask to get the material for her profile?
Before going to the interview she will research her subject, finding out about their education, their career so far, their hobbies and interests and family life. She will have read or watched any previous interviews. This background information will give her a basic picture of her subject which she can investigate in more detail. She might formulate questions about her subject's past, present and future, such as:

1. Do you have any regrets about your career moves so far?
2. Looking back, what advice can you give to someone aiming at a similar job?
3. Are you satisfied with your present position?
4. What do you like or dislike about it?
5. Is your salary enough/too much?
6. What do you think about your company's rivals?
7. What are your plans or ambitions for yourself or for your company?
8. What is your personal motto?

Her research has already given her basic information. The interview gives her a chance to find out his opinions, hopes, ambitions and goals, all of which will be combined into an in-depth feature.

A City reporter will probably already be a qualified journalist with experience of news reporting, but will not need a financial qualification – just a good understanding of how the economy and the financial sectors of Britain and other countries work.

Freelance travel writer

This is often seen as one of the most glamorous jobs in journalism, but travel writing is extremely demanding with little time for lazing on a beach.

The travel writer in our example is a freelance. He will come up with his own ideas for travel articles; for example, family holidays in Ireland. Then he will approach travel editors on newspapers and magazines to see whether they are interested in commissioning it. Having got someone interested, he will approach the tourist board or other parties interested in promoting tourism in Ireland – say, the national airline. They may agree to give him free accommodation or travel.

Although it sounds simple, our writer finds selling his work quite tough. There are many other travel writers competing for the limited space in publications. Some of his features that did make it are as follows:

- a 2,000-word article for the travel supplement of a Sunday newspaper about Borneo

- a piece with the headline 'The Insider's Guide To London' for an airline magazine

- and a piece of about 400 words on Barcelona for a women's magazine which ran as part of a series about favourite cities.

For each article he travelled to the area, sometimes paying part or all of his costs himself, did a great deal of sight-seeing and note-taking and spoke to locals such as restaurant owners, people on the street and tourist bosses. Before setting off he researched the area he was travelling to by using guide books and information sent him by the local tourist authority. He also took photographs while on each trip, in the form of colour transparencies, and offered these to travel editors as part of a package.

Travel writing is open to all, even those without journalistic experience, but it is a precarious way to make a living. Only original ideas are likely to make it into print.

Anyone thinking of travel writing as a career goal should become qualified in basic journalism first, so that if necessary they can move into other fields such as news reporting or general feature writing.

Freelance motoring correspondent

Our motoring expert is also a freelance journalist, but in the broadcast media as well as in print. Because he is freelance, he has several strands to his working life.

- He presents a half-hour local **radio** show on a Friday afternoon; his material includes interviewing guests about various aspects of motoring, tips for drivers and information on the best deals for car-buyers.

- He also presents a **television** programme, broadcast nationwide. In it, he road-tests new models, interviews guests such as the Transport Minister or a high-ranking executive from a car manufacturing company, and reports news of interest to the motorist.

- Once he became known as a motoring specialist, he started being asked to appear on other television and radio programmes in the role of **expert**. For instance, when plans for future road-building were announced by the government, our motoring correspondent was interviewed on several news programmes. He was asked his opinion of the plans – would they make life better for Britain's millions of drivers?

- His expertise has also earned him a column in a Saturday **magazine supplement** which comes with one of the national, broadsheet newspapers. He uses the column to write wittily about the experiences of the ordinary driver.

- He has written several **books** on motoring and has plans for more.

The job of motoring correspondent would be open to any journalist who wanted to apply for it. But you would need a good knowledge of, and interest in, the car industry as well as the usual journalistic skills. The best route into motoring journalism would be to apply to one of the specialist magazines.

Political correspondent, network television

This journalist has one of the most coveted jobs in the profession, reporting on politics for national television. She works from special studios near the Houses of Parliament. What might her working day contain?

- She reports live on the events of the day from both the House of Commons and the Lords. She often faces a tight deadline – when a debate continues into the late evening she many have only minutes to compile a report before it is broadcast live.

- She also interviews politicians at all levels – from a backbench MP who has rebelled against the Party Whip to a Cabinet Minister. Sometimes interviews will be done, with little warning or preparation, at Westminster; at other times they will be in the studio.

- She will attend briefings by the Press secretaries of Party leaders and senior ministers to get off-the-record information which will form the basis of stories.

- During elections, she will follow politicians on the campaign trail, interviewing them and reporting their activities to attempt to give viewers a flavour of what it was really like at the grass roots. She will also report from Party conferences.

- She will script filmed reports. For example, a Private Member's Bill may be proposed to change the laws on shop opening hours. Before it is voted on, our reporter is likely to write and present a short film explaining the issue which could then be broadcast on the early or mid-evening news.

- It is vital for her to develop contacts among MPs and Ministers. She will spend a good deal of time in the bars and tea rooms of Westminster chatting to MPs, their researchers and Press aides, other journalists and professional lobbyists.

A prerequisite of this job is an extremely good knowledge of both domestic and foreign current affairs and of how Britain's political system works, as well as journalistic experience.

Royal reporter, daily newspaper

He works for a large provincial morning paper. His brief is to cover anything and everything to do with the royal family. His primary need is good contacts among courtiers, friends and the more distant relatives of the Windsors.

In the few years that he has been doing this job he has written many front page stories – the breaking down of royal marriages, debates about the Succession and the future of the monarchy, the birth of royal children, a dramatic fire which destroyed one palace, and controversy which led to changes in the royal finances such as the paying of income tax.

His paper, and some of the stories he has written, have been heavily criticised by members of the royal family. They have issued downright denials about some of the stories he has produced, but he has eventually been proved right. Whenever he has been given a tip-off about something concerning a royal, he has carefully checked it with several other people before putting it on paper.

As well as his journalism, he is also a prolific author. He has written biographies on several royals, each based on information given him over the years by contacts.

Any news writer could aspire to becoming a royal-watcher. The special attribute you would need is the ability to move in the circles of people who surround the monarchy. Employment is mostly with newspapers at the popular end of the market and with magazines or the Press Association. Occasionally there would be the opportunity to make a television or radio documentary.

Fashion assistant, women's magazine

A job for a trainee or young journalist, the fashion assistant would work to the fashion editor. She might be helping to arrange photo shoots, style them – that is, choose the clothes, make-up and hairstyles – and then write a fashion piece for the magazine.

As she gains experience she could:

- Originate ideas for fashion articles.

- Attend the major catwalk shows in Paris, Milan, New York and London and report on them.

- Interview designers for feature pieces.

- Sub-edit copy, write material for picture captions and write headlines.

- Check finished page proofs of fashion articles.

Fashion journalism demands an interest in clothes, design and popular trends, the ability to travel and to mix with everyone from the public relations officer for a High Street chain to a designer at the head of a Paris couture house. A knowledge of fashion history is obviously useful.

Economics correspondent, national news agency
This journalist works for a large news agency supplying local newspapers and radio stations.

He covers a wide range of financial news. The source of a story might be the stock market, government measures which will affect the economy, activities of the European Commission, the Budget, the banks, the building societies, statistics such as unemployment figures and events in economies abroad.

His recent stories include:

- Covering a merger of two large building societies.

- Interviewing the Chancellor of the Exchequer about the prospect of an interest rate rise.

- Writing a feature on how likely Europe is to adopt a single currency.

- Reporting on new figures showing a downward trend in consumer spending.

- Working as part of a team reporting on the collapse of a City bank, after a trader working alone lost millions on one of the overseas stock markets.

An economics degree would obviously be useful to any journalist wanting to specialise in this area, although not essential. Practical knowledge, journalistic experience and the ability to get on with people at a high level in politics and business would be more important.

Sub-editor, Teletext
Sub-editors work in every medium – television, radio, magazines and newspapers – but our example is a sub-editor working on

Teletext, the information service provided by most television channels. BBC and ITV led the way with teletext services, but now Sky and many other satellite channels provide it too.

Because Teletext is transmitted throughout the day and night, he works on a shift basis covering nights and weekends. His job is to edit or rewrite reports from correspondents to a predetermined style and length.

- He checks the accuracy of the report and ensures it leaves no questions unanswered; it must be summed up in only a few paragraphs and easy to read on the television screen.

- He gives the report a headline, of less than half a dozen words, which will also be used in the index.

- The material he edits could be anything from a traffic update to a dramatic news story. One day he may be editing cricket dispatches from Australia in the morning and the obituary of a foreign country's Prime Minister in the afternoon. Teletext covers a wide variety of news, including domestic, foreign, sport, business and travel.

- The sub-editors report to a chief-sub, who allocates the workload and revises the finished report before transmission. Some sub-editors may specialise in certain areas, for instance foreign news, but the team on duty is not always large enough to allow this.

- Our sub may also get the opportunity to do some writing, as well as editing. For instance, he may review a film or a play and write it up for broadcast.

Basic training in journalism would equip you for this type of job, although you would need to be particularly good at writing a précis of hundreds of words very quickly. Because text is received on a television screen, space is inevitably limited. You will also need a wide knowledge of current affairs at home and abroad, so that you are able to edit any story, and know how to check facts quickly, for example in reference books.

Picture editor, news agency
The picture editor's job is to run a department of photographers. He must judge photographs on their technical and artistic merits and decide what is newsworthy.

In our example, the picture editor is employed by a news agency in the south east of England. He reports to the agency's editor and has five photographers working for him. He decides which events should be covered, briefs photographers, selects several stills from their finished film, checks the photographer's caption, makes sure the picture has been legally obtained (for example, it is against the law to take pictures in the precincts of a court of law) and offers the pictures to newspapers and magazines.

He is an organiser, making sure he has a photographer in the right place at the right time, and also a good judge of what will be of interest to a certain publication. A photograph of a motorway crash involving several vehicles may sell to a national newspaper. Pictures of particularly appealing pets may do better with a magazine. A shot of a celebrity caught off guard while out shopping may go to the local evening newspaper or even a Sunday paper.

He can offer pictures exclusively to one publication or make them available to all – he must decide which is likely to be most profitable for the agency. He will also need a good eye for how a picture will look once printed – will it be more appealing in black and white or in colour, better on newsprint or on glossy paper? Perhaps it would make a cover picture for a magazine, in which case it will command a high fee.

An experienced journalist with an interest in photography could apply for this job. He or she would need good news judgement, the ability to organise and lead other staff and to make decisions quickly and some knowledge of newspaper and magazine design and printing.

Other areas in which journalists can specialise:

Agriculture	Gardening
Architecture	Industry
Ballet	Local government
Business	Medicine
Crime	Pop music
Defence	Property
Diplomatic affairs	Religious affairs
Education	Science
Environment	Technology

But remember, almost all journalists begin by news reporting because the basic training equips them to go on to many other jobs.

3

Inside a Newspaper

'There is, of course, a certain amount of drudgery in newspaper work, just as there is in teaching classes, tunnelling into a bank or being President of the United States.'

James Thurber

'For an industry that is often said to be in terminal decline or about to be destroyed by the Internet, newspapers are showing a remarkable talent for buoyant survival. On most weekdays last year (1994) the British bought more than 14 million national newspapers and 5.5 million regional morning and evening newspapers. We still read more newspapers than almost any other nation on earth.'

Brian Macarthur, *The Times*

HOW IS A NATIONAL NEWSPAPER ORGANISED?

What is a typical day like on a national, daily newspaper? There is no 'typical' day, because news is unpredictable. Some days are hectic, others are quiet.

Some events can be anticipated. Editors know when a certain Bill will be debated in Parliament or when a royal tour will begin. They know when a court case is due to start or when an election will be held.

Other events cannot be predicted. An earthquake in China or the sudden resignation of a world leader will take everyone by surprise. Each day is a mixture of the expected and the unexpected.

How can newspapers cope with a sudden big story? Because staff work as a team, with everyone knowing exactly what his or her area of responsibility is.

How does a story get into the newspaper?
(See Figure 2.)

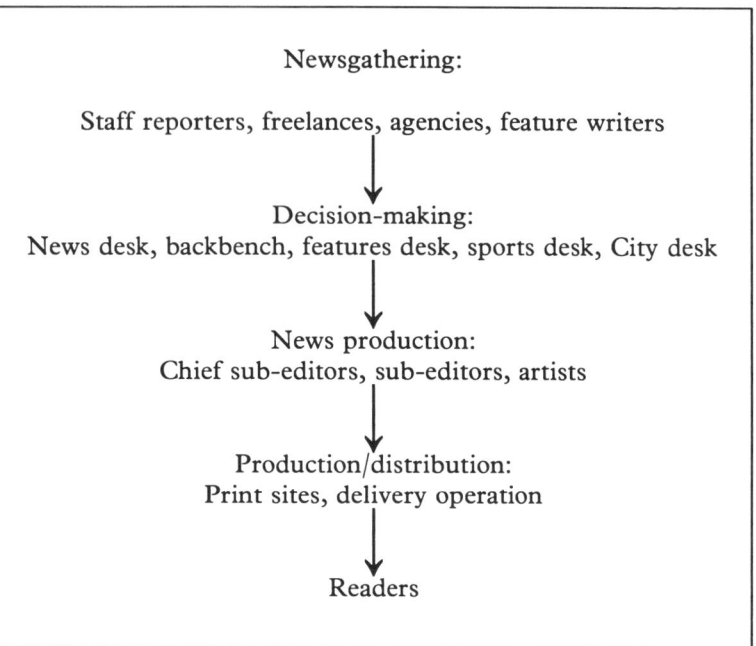

Fig. 2. Copy flow in a regional morning newspaper.

- Copy can begin its life almost anywhere. A reporter could write it in the office, or on a laptop computer at an event; it could be filed to head office from a district office or from a correspondent abroad, or be sent in by an agency.

- Almost all copy now flows into a newspaper's computer system and is read, rewritten or edited on screen. Much of the copy will go to the **newsdesk**.

- Journalists on the newsdesk will filter news copy to see if it is suitable for their paper. If so it will go to the **backbench**.

- Feature copy will go to the **features desk**.

- Copy for the **sports desk** will go straight into their computer queue. So will that for the **City desk** and for other special departments.

- The backbench or features desk will then decide, in consultation with the paper's senior executive, which stories are to go where.

- The copy will be passed to a chief sub-editor. He will allocate it to a sub-editor who will work on it and return it.

- After final checking, it will go into a computer queue for typesetting.

- Whole pages will be typeset at once and faxed to the print sites.

EXAMPLE: THE *DAILY EXPRESS*

As an example of how a national newspaper functions, we will look at the *Daily Express*. Of course, different newspapers have different working practices, but the general principles are similar.

The *Daily Express* has a circulation of almost 1.3 million copies a day and is aimed at the 'middle market', that is, readers wanting more than a tabloid such as the *Daily Mirror* but less than a broadsheet such as *The Times*.

This is its **editorial team**:

- Editor.
- Deputy editor plus other very senior journalists with titles such as Executive Editor or Associate Editor.
- Assistant editors who are senior journalists, each responsible for one area such as sport, news, features, politics, design and promotions.

The rest of the journalists are assigned to clearly defined **desks** or departments. Some of these are: news, features, sport, finance, women's interest, art and design, diary, politics, foreign, showbusiness and production.

Every desk is led by a section editor, who has a deputy and one or more assistants. Each department has a team of newsgatherers – reporters or feature writers – and production staff.

How a desk works

The section editor is in overall charge, reporting directly to the paper's editor. He or she decides which stories should be covered and where they will be placed in the paper. The journalists working on the desk make sure those decisions are carried out and supervise both the writing and editing of copy.

Newsgathering

The journalists on the desk brief reporters and feature writers and commission news stories or features from freelances. They decide how many words a story or feature should be, tell writers the time by which it must be filed and keep tabs on what progress is being made in getting information and interviews.

News production

The desk journalists are also in charge of production. They supervise layout artists who design pages, choose pictures, send copy to sub-editors to be worked on, read finished page proofs and ensure each page is 'locked' (or completed) on deadline.

The different departments have clearly defined tasks, as described below.

The newsdesk: bringing in the news

This desk is led by a **news editor** and staffed by a team of experienced journalists. One is responsible for foreign news, another for regional news.

The newsdesk's jobs are to:

- Decide which events will be covered.
- Brief reporters on which stories to work on, where to go, who to interview and what questions to ask them.
- Liaise with reporters who are out of the office throughout the working day.
- Liaise with specialist writers.

The newsdesk has a number of **reporters** and **correspondents** working for it. Most work in head office, but some, known as district reporters, are in offices around the country.

The foreign news editor also has a team of reporters working for him, based in major cities abroad, such as Washington, Paris, Beijing and Moscow.

All these journalists are staff employees, but the newsdesk may also use **freelances**. For example, if a story breaks in a remote part of Scotland, it may be quicker to send a local freelance to cover it than to fly a staff person up from Glasgow or London. Similarly, there are many, many locations abroad where a local freelance is on the spot and which it would take hours for a staff journalist to reach.

The news editor and his staff spend much time on the phone to members of the public who feel they have a story to tell, to freelances with a story to sell and to press and public relations officers with a product or a personality to push.

The backbench: producing the news pages

Reports and pictures flow in from various sources. It is on the backbench that they are transformed into finished pages.

The **night editor** is in charge and has several senior journalists working with him. He decides, in consultation with the editor, which reports and pictures will be used and where they should go in the paper.

These are some of the backbench tasks:

- Read and evaluate all the copy that arrives on screen.
- Raise queries with reporters if necessary.
- Make sure each report is fair, accurate, legal and clearly written.
- Write headlines.
- Select photographs to accompany stories.
- Brief designers on each page to be laid out.
- Read finished page proofs.

Throughout the working day the night editor is involved in conferences to discuss breaking news events.

The backbench passes copy to the chief news sub-editor and a team of around 30 'subs' all working on screen. Each sub is allocated a number of stories to work on. They edit the copy, write picture captions and headlines, then return it to the chief sub.

When he has 'revised' it – checked that it is well written, has a good headline and fits into its alloted space – he will file it to a computer queue for typesetting. Whole pages will then be typeset at once.

Backbench journalists and subs are highly experienced. They will probably have worked on provincial papers as reporters and subs before moving to a national paper.

Features desk: handling everything except news and sport

The **features editor** and a team of experienced journalists commission material for and produce all pages which are not news or sport.

Some of their pages are used for comment, opinion and in-depth analysis, some for general features on lifestyle, entertainment and popular culture. Examples would be a lengthy interview with a film celebrity who has recently won an Oscar; an article about a new play or television drama; an interview with a leading politician or a promotion in which the paper is giving away substantial prizes.

The work of the features desk is to:

- Brief staff writers and columnists.
- Commission articles from freelances.
- Read all incoming copy, checking it as the backbench do the news copy.
- Brief designers on pages to be laid out.
- Select photographs.
- Read finished page proofs.
- Originate ideas for future features.
- Serialise books, adapting the text, choosing illustrations and getting pages designed.

This department also has its own team of sub-editors.

The leader writer: forming opinion

He writes the paper's opinion column, regarded as one of the most important items in its pages. It is written in direct consultation with the editor, who will want to ensure that his own views are reflected.

The City desk: reporting the financial world

This desk is responsible for the financial pages of the newspaper. It has a similar staff structure to the features desk, and does similar jobs. The difference is that all the news and features on these pages is financial.

There is a City editor, a deputy and writers specialising in personal finance, business news, consumer affairs, stocks and shares.

The production of the pages is carried out by a chief sub-editor and a team of subs.

The women's desk: a specialist role

Many newspapers, the *Express* among them, have a department writing material aimed at female readers. The women's editor, her deputy and two or three writers will write or commission enough articles to fill several pages a week.

The diary: a gossip column

Journalists on the 'diary' find and write stories for the gossip column which appears daily. There is a diary editor, a sub-editor and several reporters.

The travel desk: writing for the consumer
The travel editor has a team of writers and subs. Their brief is to fill the travel pages which appear in the Saturday edition. They will go on trips abroad and write features describing their experiences as well as writing news stories about travel and tourism.

The art desk: layouts, graphics and illustrations
This section designs the newspaper's pages and provides graphics and line drawings. The art director is responsible for the appearance of the paper. He dictates which typefaces are used and the style of the layout. He supervises three types of artist, those drawing layouts, those creating graphics on computer and cartoonists/illustrators. Art desk staff are rarely journalists.

The picture desk: photographs from home and abroad
The picture editor controls coverage of events and a team of photographers. This section is responsible for taking and processing news and feature pictures for every department of the newspaper. Picture researchers will also work here; their job is to track down and buy particular pictures which are required.

The legal office: limiting the risks
This is staffed by the newspaper's own team of barristers. They are not journalists but are experts in newspaper law.

They read all the copy for the newspaper, looking for risks of libel and ensuring that reports are not in contempt of court. They also consider whether rights to privacy have been observed and whether a report meets the criteria laid down in the Code of Practice issued by the Press Complaints Commission. They check photographs to ensure they are not illegal or intrusive. They also deal with complaints from the public, sometimes admitting an error and advising the editor to print a correction, at other times defending the paper for what it wrote.

Columnists: personality writers
A newspaper's character is defined by its editor and its writers. Columnists play a large part in this. Their individual style and opinions help give the newspaper characteristics which make it different from other newspapers.

The *Daily Express* has several regular columnists, including Anne Robinson and Anthony Holden.

Columnists often have a large following among readers who will change papers if the columnist does.

OTHER NATIONAL NEWSPAPERS

Like the *Express*, the other nationals have an **editorial staff** of hundreds of journalists and a contacts directory of freelances. Among the staff writers are specialists, experts in a particular field, including a political editor, a transport correspondent, an arts editor, showbusiness reporters, a books editor, a health correspondent, a shopping editor, fashion editor and motoring correspondent.

They print several different **editions** for various areas of the country. Some even change their masthead – the logo at the top of page one – for Scotland.

Some are **broadsheet** and some are **tabloid**, but they all carry a mixture of home and foreign news and features.

How many readers do they have?

Newspaper circulations are measured in copies sold, rather than number of readers. The sales figure is precise, but the number of readers would have to be estimated, assuming more than one person reads each copy.

Who sells what in Britain today? These figures (in millions) are for January 1997.

Dailies

Sun	3.939
Daily Mirror	2.407
Daily Star	0.660
Daily Mail	2.147
Daily Express	1.237
Daily Telegraph	1.142
Guardian	0.413
Times	0.766
Independent	0.253
Financial Times	0.299

Sundays

News of the World	4.533
Sunday Mirror	2.387
People	2.012

Mail on Sunday	2.122
Sunday Express	1.165
Sunday Times	1.325
Sunday Telegraph	0.897
Observer	0.467
Independent on Sunday	0.272

(*Source*: Audit Bureau of Circulation.)

COVERING THE NEWS

'When a dog bites a man, that is not news, but when a man bites a dog, that is news.'

Charles Anderson Dana, the *New York Times*, 1882

A daily newspaper's day starts at around 7am and finishes at about 4am the next day. Morning newspapers, national and regional, begin printing in late evening and continue until the early hours, but the story does not stop there. Planning for the next day begins before the last is over.

Throughout the day there are frequent conferences and informal discussions, and constant reaction to moving events.

The heart of a national newspaper is still – despite the many sections some of them carry – news.

What is newsworthy?

The answer depends on the newspaper. *The Sun* may find a story about an escaped parrot newsworthy, but *The Times* would not. The *Western Mail* might splash on a story about corruption among members of a Cardiff council, but it could make only a filler (one paragraph story) for *The Guardian*. All newspapers have their own news agenda.

Yet it is still possible to define news. It is a story that has one or more of these qualities:

- It is **dramatic** – an event causing excitement or astonishment.
- It is **unexpected** – surprising or shocking.
- It is **significant** – meaning it may affect others or bring about change.
- It involves **personalities** – well-known or powerful figures.

Diary of a news day

The diary on pages 58 and 59 shows how the news is covered. The

Diary of a national newspaper

7am: Newsdesk staff arrive and begin planning coverage. They compile a list of events that may make stories for the next morning's edition – the **schedule**. Sources of news include:

- the morning newspapers
- future diary of events
- reporters and correspondents at home and abroad
- television and radio bulletins
- other publications, such as current affairs magazines
- tips from contacts
- news agencies, including wire services
- press releases

9.30am: Features staff arrive; begin planning and commissioning features for the next day's edition and for future editions.

9.30–10am: Reporters and other writers arrive and are given assignments. Some may have to travel abroad or hundreds of miles in Britain, but still meet an early evening deadline.

10.30am: Morning conference. This is attended by all the senior executives and department heads. The news, features, sports and picture editors will each provide a schedule of the day's activities ahead. These will be read out and discussed. The editor may say that he or she likes a particular idea or does not want another pursued.

By the end of the meeting, all section editors will know which stories their staff are to work on. They may have to contact freelances or experts to assist with articles. The picture editor will send his photographers out and graphics artists will begin work on tables and diagrams.

From 10am: Reporters, photographers, feature writers, columnists, the leader writer and many other staff prepare stories, features and pictures for the edition. Others fix up interviews for future editions.

12 noon: Night editor begins planning news pages. Meeting with the editor to take early decisions on which stories to use where.

1.30pm: Sub-editors and other backbench staff arrive. Begin reading and checking copy, roughly editing it and laying out pages.

4pm: Afternoon conference. This is the crucial meeting at which the shape of the edition is decided. Senior executives are present. The night editor will recommend which stories and photographs should take prominence, for instance on the front page. The news, picture, feature and sports editors make progress reports on new stories breaking, how other stories are shaping up, interviews and photographs and, after discussion, the editor decides what goes in the paper and what is 'spiked'.

From 4pm until the early hours of the next morning, pages are laid out, copy edited and rewritten, page proofs checked and finished pages sent electronically to the printing centres. It will not all go smoothly to the plan decided in afternoon conference. The editor may have a change of mind or a big story may break, which means throwing out or rearranging the previous material.

Stories can be 'spiked' (held out of the paper) for legal reasons. New pictures may arrive which mean redrawing pages. For the next six hours or so the newsroom will be hectic, with every computer terminal occupied, people rushing to meet the deadline for each page, and the news constantly changing.

9.30pm: Off-stone time. This is the deadline by which all pages for the first edition must be complete, with headlines written, copy fitting and pictures in place. The phrase 'off stone' dates from the time when newspaper pages were assembled in metal, literally on a huge stone base. 'Off stone' meant the finished page could go to be printed; today it means exactly the same, although type is now set and pages sent to be printed electronically.

At 9.30pm, there is an audible sigh of relief from the entire newsroom.

There will be three more editions after the first, in which several pages will be changed each time. This is often because of sport – to put in results or fuller reports from football or cricket matches. Sometimes the purpose is to put in stories from a different region, sometimes simply to update the news.

10.30pm: First editions of rival newspapers arrive in the office. The night editor checks them for news reports and pictures which his own paper may have missed. These will then be followed up by the night shift reporters. Television news will also be monitored throughout the evening.

From now until 2am there will be constant edition changes.

2.30am: The office is almost silent, manned only by two or three staff on 'dogwatch', the day's final shift. Four editions will have been completed but, if a big story breaks, it is still possible to change the front page. This is called a 'slip' edition. Journalists on the backbench and newsdesk will monitor the agencies' output on computer screen and watch television news so they are aware of any new stories.

5am: The night log is prepared with a list of actions that need to be taken when the day staff arrive at 7am. Any problems or complaints from readers will be listed, along with the changes that were made to the paper throughout the night. There will be suggestions for stories that need following up in the morning.

And, then, another news day begins.

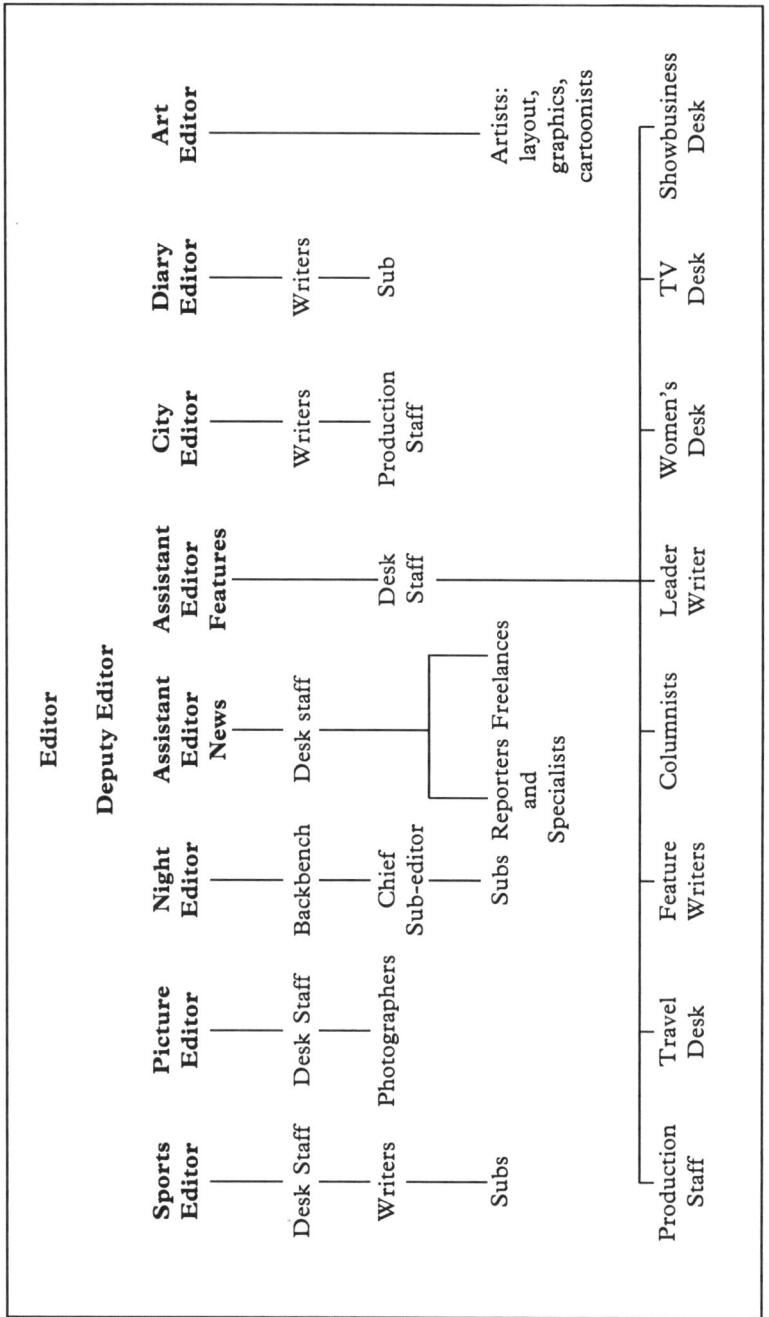

Fig. 3. Staff structure on a national newspaper.

10 March 1997
News schedule
News editor: Andrew Jenkins

- Agriculture Secretary meets farmers' representatives and RSPCA to discuss veal production and export. Parliamentary reporter.

- Couple in court charged with manslaughter of four-year-old son and arson at their home. Crime reporter.

- Trial of businessman accused of shotgun murders of his girlfriend's parents at isolated farm in Mid Glamorgan. Local freelance covering.

- Metropolitan Police launch new guide to personal safety on the streets. Staff reporter.

- GP who is also government health adviser accused of 20 offences in connection with heroin and cocaine. Medical correspondent.

- Centenary of the National Trust. Press launch attended by the Prince of Wales. Royal reporter.

- Memorial service for actor. Showbusiness reporter.

- Launch of new edition of *Guinness Book of Records*. Literary Editor covering.

- Labour Party launch of manifesto on the British constitution and devolution. Parliamentary reporter.

- Groups protesting at road-building plans from Devon to Kent plan to light bonfires, beacons and torches. District reporter.

- Airline of the Year Awards presented by *Executive Travel* magazine. Travel editor.

- Opening of new production of musical *Sunset Boulevard*. Shaftesbury Theatre. Theatre Critic.

diagram of a newspaper's staff in Figure 3 also shows how the different departments work together.

Finding the news

The image of the investigative reporter is one of the most glamorous in journalism. Working undercover, he or she traps a prominent politician into confessing to a scandal or discovers corruption in a multinational company.

This is the exception and newspapers get most of their stories in less exciting ways. A journalist is just as likely to be sent to cover a routine event as a dramatic news story.

Diary and off-diary stories

News is broken down into diary and off-diary events.

Diary events are those which are expected and which the news editor thinks may produce good copy. Every newspaper and local radio newsroom has a diary of such routine events – courts, tribunals and council meetings.

Many other events are also known about in advance; for example, a visit to a city by a prominent figure or member of the royal family, or a top sporting fixture.

Off-diary events are the unexpected – a train crash or a sudden resignation. News editors hear about these from various sources – the police, local authorities and contacts – and respond quickly, sending a reporter and/or a photographer to the scene.

News schedule for the *Daily Planet*

Let's assume that someone has started a new morning newspaper, circulating nationally. The schedule on page 61 shows some of the stories that would appear in it.

Capturing the unusual stories

Newspapers like their share of humorous stories, and reporters can find themselves covering more off-beat happenings than those on the daily diary. Here are some examples:

- A virus is sweeping through a variety of the petunia plant that is a favourite with Britain's gardeners.

- A cosmetics company claims that a new cream will slim inches off the thighs.

- A caffeine chewing gum has been launched for those who don't have time to make a cup of coffee.

- Bottled mineral water has been exposed as indistinguishable from tap water and a waste of money.

- Open-air opera performances at a stately home have been banned because they are disturbing residents in a nearby village.

PROVINCIAL NEWSPAPERS

How are local newspapers different?

There are some similarities between national and provincial newspapers. Their **working methods** are similar – reporters go out on stories, sub-editors work on the copy in the office – although this is changing (see below).

Their **staffing structure** is along the same lines, but much simpler.

Staff numbers are also much smaller. The actual size of the staff depends on the size of the paper's circulation and the number of editions. Some small weeklies may have fewer than a dozen journalists, some large regional evenings could have fifty or more.

They **find news** in much the same way as national newspapers do, from contacts, from their own reporters and freelances, from lists of court cases or the agendas for council meetings, from other media such as local radio news bulletins, by compiling a schedule of daily events and by being tipped off about sudden, dramatic events.

Apart from staffing levels, the main difference is their **news agenda**. Local news, features and sport fills most of their pages, although they may have one or two pages for national and foreign news.

The changing face of the newsroom

Up until the mid-1990s, local newspapers were mini versions of the bigger, bolder national papers. Then an alternative way of working began to emerge. The question was asked: 'Why do we have to have different people to do different jobs, such as reporters to gather the news and sub-editors to edit, cut and check it?'

Some newspapers began to break down the barriers between jobs.

- One result was at *The Journal* in Newcastle and the *Press and Journal* in Aberdeen. There, the two posts of news editor and features editor were abolished and replaced with one post, head of content.

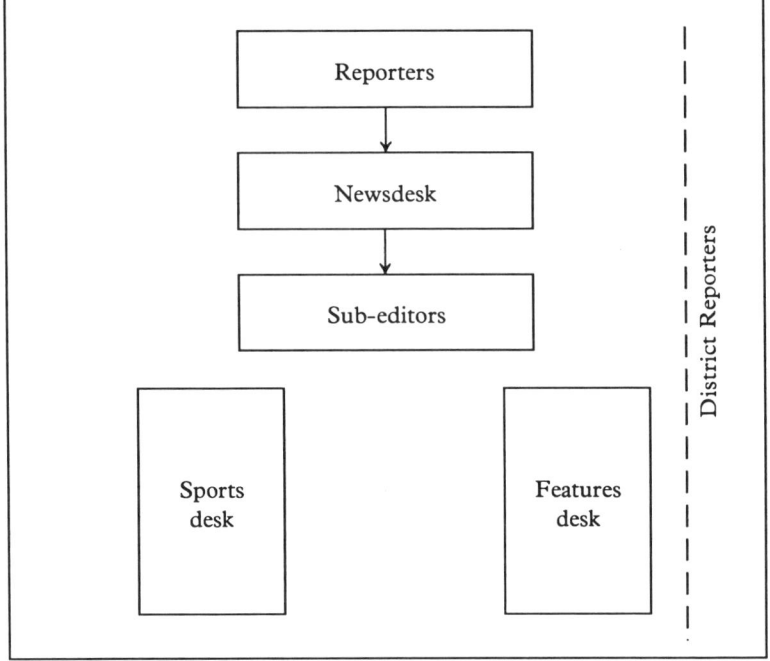

Fig. 4. A traditional provincial newspaper newsroom.

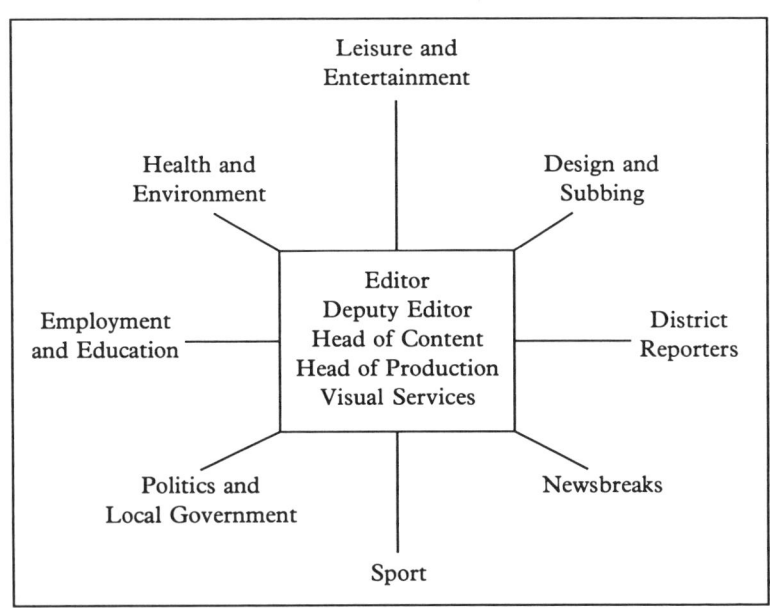

Fig. 5. An orbital newsroom.

- At the *Yorkshire Evening Post* in Leeds, the features department has been absorbed into the news department.

- At the *Evening Advertiser* in Swindon, journalists are grouped into 'pods', or units.

- The *Basildon Evening Echo* has 'multi-functional' teams of journalists who see projects through from an initial idea to print.

- And the *Telegraph and Argus* in Bradford has what it describes as an 'orbital' newsroom, with writers, subs, 'visual services' such as picture desk and graphics all integrated physically. There is also less hierarchy than in an old-style newsroom. (See Figures 4 and 5.)

The model of the future is of small teams of journalists sitting in a 'loop' around the editor. Writers may write their copy, pull up a story shape created by a layout sub, and either cut or expand it to fit; journalists may also 'scan' pictures into pages. Newspapers are already travelling down the road to multi-skilling.

Where are local newspapers going?

Provincial papers have a mix of news, but the trend is towards more coverage of local affairs. Journalists are increasingly expected to get to know the community in which they work.

An executive of one of Britain's major provincial newspaper publishing groups, Westminster Press, points out that: 'Local papers do best when they are local, and many of them are less local now.' Nicholas Herbert, the retiring deputy chief executive, also told the journalists' magazine, *UK Press Gazette*, that he believed that readers want more detail and 'more bite'.

Rachael Campey, editor of the *Express & Echo* in Exeter, comments that: 'If we are to provide the sort of content our readers want to go on reading, the journalists' contact with, and interest in, them and their community has to be more than skin deep.'

How many do they sell?

These are a selection of the many regional newspapers; circulation figures are for July–December 1996.

Glasgow Evening Times (Mon-Fri)	139,762
Aberdeen Press and Journal	104,901

Huddersfield Daily Examiner	36,406
Bristol Evening Post (Mon–Fri)	83,048
East Anglian Daily Times (Ipswich)	47,951
Northern Echo (Darlington)	69,370
Manchester Evening News (Mon–Fri)	171,463
Reading Evening Post	23,013
Sunday Mercury (Birmingham)	145,046
Gloucestershire Citizen	34,925
Yorkshire Post	75,528
Leicester Mercury	113,417
Southend Evening Echo	44,579
Sunday Sun (Newcastle)	118,960

(Source: Audit Bureau of Circulation.)

CASE STUDIES

The national newspaper news reporter

Alex, 37, has always enjoyed being 'on the road', rather than transferring to a desk job.

He began work on an evening newspaper in the north. He started out reporting the staples of all local newspapers – council meetings, local campaigns, human interest stories about local people. He was quickly promoted to news editor, and then to editor.

But he disliked the administrative side of the job and preferred being out of the office, reporting from the grass roots. Alex decided to move to London and, for a while, was a freelance reporter working on several national newspapers.

He gained a reputation for being prepared to work hard, put in long hours and not give up easily and he was soon offered a staff post.

During his five years with a national paper he has investigated and reported several major stories. One was an exposé of the behaviour of a Cabinet Minister who had been paid by a wealthy industrialist to lobby on his behalf. Another was the case of the chief executive of a major public corporation who had been using legal loopholes to avoid paying income tax. Both stories made the paper's lead and ran for several days.

During the past year, Alex has also covered the following stories:

- Reporting the trial of an IRA bomber which took place at the Central Criminal Court in London. The trial lasted three and a half weeks and Alex was present every day, Monday to Friday, sitting in the Press area from around 10am to around 6pm. Each day he would talk to his newsdesk at about lunchtime to tell them what the day's evidence was likely to be, and thus how good a story he would have. Then he filed his report for the first edition at about 5pm, with an updated report later.

- Covering the story of the marriage breakdown of a well-known television presenter. Alex got a tip-off from a contact that the man was to move out of his country home and into a London flat with another woman. He 'doorstepped' the country house (the unglamorous job of standing around outside waiting for either the man or his wife to emerge) for eighteen hours. Eventually the television personality did come out, laden with suitcases, but refused to comment to Alex. Rather than give up, he wrote to the celebrity's wife, asking for an interview, which she granted.

- Flying to France to report on a British holiday coach which had crashed in the mountains. Getting the story involved talking to survivors, eyewitnesses, the driver, French police, local residents and other emergency services.

- Interviewing a well-known footballer who had admitted to a drug addiction and gambling debts, and writing his story. Alex got a wider perspective by talking to the footballer's wife and friends.

The aspects of the job he most enjoys are being out of the office, talking to all sorts of people, travelling and piecing together the different elements of a story until he has found out exactly what has happened. He says: 'It's like doing a complicated jigsaw in very little time.'

The foreign editor

David, 40, has been with his national newspaper for eighteen years, having started with the paper as a news reporter. After a few years he joined the newsdesk as an assistant news editor, which involved working in head office and helping to direct reporters about the coverage of stories.

He had various other duties while working on the newsdesk – helping compile the daily diary, planning the coverage of future events, interviewing potential staff reporters, dealing with payments to correspondents and freelances.

Three years ago he was appointed Foreign Editor. He is now in charge of all the paper's **foreign correspondents**. They are made up of those on staff, paid a salary, working in major cities such as New York, Washington, Tokyo, Beijing, Moscow, Paris and Brussels. Other countries are covered by freelance correspondents, paid a retainer so that they are available when needed. He has access to a large number of freelances in many cities including Berlin, Rome, Amsterdam, Los Angeles, Sydney and Hong Kong.

The working day

- David arrives at the office at 7.30am. He reads all the morning newspapers and watches breakfast television to discover which foreign stories will need covering. Then he compiles his schedule, showing the foreign stories of the day in order of importance.

- Next, he begins talking to his reporters by telephone (allowing for time differences) or sends them a message by computer. Each will be briefed on the story he would like them to do, and he will tell them how many words he wants. He may also ask them to make enquiries about photographs.

- Throughout the day David will keep in touch with his reporters, monitoring the progress of each story. He will also receive calls from other staff or freelance reporters who have a story which they think might make the night's edition. David will also attend both morning and afternoon conference, when decisions about what will go into the edition are made.

- When reporters file their copy (by telephone, computer or, rarely, by fax), David will read it and may either edit it, rewrite it or send it back to the reporter for amendments. He will make sure that every story on his schedule is complete and in the office before he leaves, probably at about 7.30pm.

- He will have to deal with some administration during the day – queries over payments or expenses from reporters working abroad.

- He will also find time to read current affairs magazines such as *Time* and *Newsweek* for information on world events.

He enjoys his job because of his interest in different cultures. He says: 'I feel I'm seeing a lot of the world without ever leaving the office.'

The evening newspaper trainee

Tim is 20 and has been on the paper for nine months. He joined after A-levels and is on a two-year traineeship.

After the first week, when he went out on stories with several senior reporters to get a feel for the job, he says he knew he was hooked. Since then he has covered a wide variety of news events, written features, reported on local football matches, reviewed performances at the town's theatre and given a talk on journalism at his old school.

Some of the stories he has most enjoyed doing include:

- Discovering an encampment of 'travellers' just outside the town and writing a news story and a feature about their lifestyle. Tim got the story first after seeing their vans and lorries moving in on his way to work. There was a strong local reaction after his story went to press, from residents and local government officials, making two follow-up stories.

- Interviewing older residents for a series about memories of VE Day, the day the Second World War ended in Europe.

- Writing a light-hearted travel feature about a canal holiday taken with a group of friends.

- Being part of a team reporting local government elections; this meant interviewing candidates, going to different areas of the town to write 'colour' pieces before the election; phoning results through to the newsdesk on the night; and going back to the places he visited earlier to get reaction to the result after the election.

Tim has also covered some of the town's soccer fixtures and eventually hopes to move into sports reporting.

The showbusiness writer

Angela is a graduate trainee on a national newspaper. She has a two-year contract to work for the paper, during which she will be trained at its expense. Then, she may or may not be given a staff job.

During her tenure she will work in several departments but has started with showbusiness. So far she has interviewed several minor actors and actresses, a film director and a television producer. She also writes reviews of television programmes and previews of others.

One of her regular tasks is to generate a small feature to accompany the paper's radio programme listing, under the title 'Radio Pick of the Day'. It is her responsibility to choose a programme and write about it. Her daily slot is about 300 words. Angela has also accompanied senior writers when they have interviewed important celebrities, simply to gain experience.

In a few weeks she will move to sport, where she will report on various events. After that she will spend time on the sub-editors' desk, on the Diary section and finally as a writer on the Women's Desk.

She says the advantage of coming in as a graduate trainee is that she is experiencing several different departments, which will help her in deciding what she eventually wants to do.

4

Working in Magazines

'To run a successful magazine company you need three things; first, well-focused editors, second, sharp managements who have a very clear idea of what each magazine is trying to do and third, a publisher who acts as a kind of business manager. Every day I speak to virtually every editor and publisher twice.'

Nicholas Coleridge, editorial director, *Condé Nast*

'Business magazines, particularly weeklies, have strong news sections. The reporting that they carry is of a high standard and they frequently break stories before the nationals. Journalists from business magazines often move on to national newspapers or TV.'

A Career in Magazines, Periodicals Training Council

WHAT IS A MAGAZINE?

A magazine – or periodical – is any publication that is published periodically. There are more than 7,000 periodicals circulating in Britain. Some you will see on every news-stand. Others are sold by subscription or have 'controlled circulations', that is, they are sent to a carefully targeted group, such as doctors or dentists. Some are general interest, others specialist.

There is a magazine available on almost every subject. They range from the well-known **consumer** titles covering fashion, do-it-yourself, cookery, cars and interior design to titles aimed at a **trade** or profession. An example of the latter category is the *UK Press Gazette*, for journalists.

There are also **house** magazines produced by large companies, usually for their staff; **specialist** titles dedicated to one subject, such as *Athletics Weekly*; **current affairs** magazines such as *Time* and *The Spectator*; and magazine **supplements** with many daily and Sunday newspapers.

About 2,500 consumer titles exist and about 4,500 business, trade and technical magazines. Here are some examples:

Consumer magazines

Good Housekeeping, Cosmopolitan, Which?, Tatler, Harpers & Queen, Radio Times, GQ, Chat, Vanity Fair, Country Living, Hello, Vogue. Those aimed at children and young adults include *Sugar, Smash Hits, Just Seventeen, 19, Mizz* and *Loaded*.

Business and professional

Campaign (the advertising industry), *Construction News* (the building industry), *Computer Weekly, Computing, Flight International* (the aviation industry), *Personal Computer World, The Stage* (the entertainment industry), *The Grocer* (retail businesses).

House magazines

These are magazines produced specifically for one company or organisation and the circulation is limited to employees or members. Examples are *Export Today*, the journal of the Institute of Export, and *Barclays News*, the staff magazine of the Barclays Bank Group.

Specialist magazines

These cover a specific area of interest and include *Horse & Hound, Angling Times, Yachting World, Motorcycle News, Auto Express* and *New Scientist*.

Best-sellers: magazine circulations

Circulations obviously vary hugely. At the top end are *Readers' Digest* and the *Radio Times* with circulations of more than a million, while at the bottom end there are specialist titles printing just a few hundred copies. The following figures are for January–June 1996.

Reader's Digest	1,765,000
Radio Times	1,405,862
Good Housekeeping	489,239
Cosmopolitan	460,141
Marie Claire	452,521
Loaded	238,955
Smash Hits	202,202
Just Seventeen	162,490
Esquire	107,058

WHAT JOBS EXIST?

All magazines employ journalists, some staff, some freelance. They take on either school-leavers with A-levels or graduates and train them on the job, or employ trained journalists.

For anyone trying to get their first job in magazine journalism, it is worth remembering that graduates are increasingly preferred. Training by employer is not guaranteed: the recession of the early 1990s led to many courses being discontinued, although they may start again as prospects improve.

Specialist titles are more likely to recruit those with a knowledge of their particular area. Some ask for journalistic experience, others do not.

All magazines use a percentage of freelance material so journalists who cannot immediately get a staff job may still be able to sell their work.

A growing area of journalism

A career in magazine journalism is worth pursuing if only because the number of magazines, and therefore the opportunities for employment, is growing. The Periodical Publishers Association estimates that the number of titles grew by 73 per cent in the ten years ending 1995. The industry's directory, *British Rates and Data* (*BRAD*), listed more than 7,700 titles in 1995.

One area that has expanded rapidly in the 1990s is the men's lifestyle market, including titles such as *Loaded*, *XL* and *Men's Health*. Another growth area is the technology and lifestyle titles, such as *Wired* and *Internet*.

WHAT DO MAGAZINE JOURNALISTS DO?

Working in magazines has many similarities with newspapers. Journalists research and write news stories and features, interview both ordinary people and celebrities, sub-edit copy and write headlines.

The crucial **difference** is that magazines do not have the immediacy of daily newspapers, nor the tight deadlines. However, on some magazines, such as weekly titles with a high news content, the pace will be almost that of a newspaper office. Writers will face strict deadlines, although weekly rather than daily.

A special problem with magazines is the '**lead in**', the time between all editorial copy and pictures being completed and printing. Because of colour printing, this can be several days. For example, one supplement issued with a daily newspaper on Saturday has to be 'off stone' by the previous Tuesday evening. Magazine journalists must always think ahead. Will the story still be relevant four or five days after being written? Are any of the facts likely to change? Could an event be cancelled or postponed?

Other magazines have a **monthly deadline**, and an even longer 'lead in'. Work is prepared carefully so that it is not out of date by the time it is printed. But a monthly deadline also allows more time for researching and writing an article, for finding case histories, interviewing people, tracking down photographs or illustrations – and for worrying about whether any other magazine will do a similar feature before yours is on the news-stands.

What sort of stories do they carry?

Because of the frequency with which they are published – weekly, monthly, quarterly – magazines put less emphasis on news and more on features. However, some business journals are the only publications covering news in their area, and give it several pages.

There is no hard and fast rule. The content of any magazine will be dictated by various factors, but mainly by the target readership. Any magazine editor will ask: what do my readers want in this publication? The answer will largely shape the product.

Keeping standards high

Magazine journalists work to the same standards as newspaper journalists. Copy, be it an article about interior decorating or a page of beauty tips, must be clearly written, accurate, fair and unlikely to give rise to a libel action.

Much as on newspapers, editors direct their department heads who brief writers and sub-editors, photographers and designers.

Magazines offer more scope than newspapers for writing elegantly rather than simply reporting the facts. They also offer the chance for journalists to work wholly on a subject that interests them.

EXAMPLE: A WOMEN'S MAGAZINE

'It is hard news that catches readers. Features hold them.'

Lord Northcliffe

The women's magazine market in Britain is thriving and highly competitive. The range of publications covers all socio-economic and age groups.

Magazines are specifically targeted, for example at working women, or at those with an interest in fashion or the home; each is also aimed at a particular age group.

As our example, we will take a glossy, monthly, magazine aimed at women over 30. It concentrates on features about real women, both domestic and international, fashion, beauty, the home, relationships, health, food and drink, careers and travel.

The staff

- *Editor*: She (or he) oversees all the content and production of the magazine. She sets the publication's agenda, style and tone, deciding what sort of features to carry; takes key decisions about whether to publish controversial material; takes responsibility for keeping the magazine on budget; liaises with advertising and marketing departments; and represents the magazine to the public.

- *Deputy editor*: Does all the day-to-day running of the magazine – briefs department heads, takes editorial conferences, monitors progress of features and other content, reads copy before and after it has been subbed and liaises with designers. She also stands in for the editor.

- *Features editor*: Originates ideas; commissions articles and photographs; briefs freelancers and staff about how to write particular articles; reads raw and edited copy. She also keeps an eye on rival magazines to see what they are planning.

- *News editor*: Keeps up to date with products and services of interest to readers and writes or commissions news stories about them. Arranges testing of new products which will make the basis of future articles.

- *Fashion editor*: Suggests ideas for themed fashion spreads, organises photo shoots, chooses models, writes fashion copy. Attends major catwalk shows.

- *Family and health editor*: Tracks news on these subjects, writing small stories or long features as appropriate. Some of the subjects she might cover include nursery education, children's toys and books, medical developments, human interest stories.

- *Consumer editor*: As above, but concentrating on consumer news.

- *Production editor*: A key job on any magazine. She oversees the design and editing of all editorial pages; ensures the production schedule is met, reads page proofs, checks headlines written by sub-editors, liaises with colour production staff and printers.

- *Sub-editors*: Cut or rewrite copy, write headlines and captions.

- *Art editor*: Originates the design of the magazine, choosing typefaces and the style of the layout; designs the cover and lays out other pages. Oversees graphics and other artwork, such as logos.

- *Designers*: Lay out pages under the direction of the art editor.

- *Beauty editor*: Monitors new products and services, writing short or long pieces as appropriate. Answers readers' queries. She may also organise workshops or 'makeovers' for readers.

- *Travel editor*: Writes or commissions one lengthy travel feature and a column of 'shorts' for each issue.

- *Cookery editor*: Writes and tests recipes.

- *Wine editor*: Writes monthly column on what is available in the shops, with recommended buys.

- *Columnist*: Writes monthly piece from a personal viewpoint.

- *Contributing editors (writers)*: Write features at the direction of the editor, or features editor. Contribute their own ideas for articles.

- *Picture editor*: Arranges photo shoots, briefs photographers, buys in pictures from outside sources such as agencies, chooses pictures for use in the magazine.

How is a magazine produced?

Because of the lead in, work on each issue begins some time before publication date. In our example, a monthly magazine, it is six weeks. The monthly diary is shown on page 77:

Production diary of monthly magazine

Day one: Each issue begins with a **planning meeting**. On the agenda will be:

- *Pagination* (number of pages in the magazine).
- *Schedule of contents*. For the current issue, the magazine is planning a feature on affairs and the effect on marriages, how families cope with especially gifted children, a light-hearted piece on women who would like to swap jobs with other women, a news feature on a war between rival prostitutes in a Midlands town and two foreign articles.
- There will also be a *fashion* feature with photographs of the latest Paris collections, a feature on where to buy clothes for sport and exercise and another on health farms.
- *Also on the schedule*: a travel piece on Tuscany, with special emphasis on the region's food and wine; a page of health tips; readers' letters; columns by regular writers; a short story; new products for the home; horoscopes; readers' questions; several pages of cookery hints and menus; a wine column; guide to current films, television, theatre and books; and a consumer test of washing machines.

The meeting will be attended by the editor, deputy editor and heads of departments – features editor, fashion, beauty, consumer, cookery, art, and production editors. The advertising and marketing departments will also be present.

Week one
Heads of departments will commission articles, either from staff writers (contributing editors) or from freelances. The picture editor will begin organising photo shoots or negotiating to buy photographs.

The *advertising department* will negotiate with the editor a 'flat plan', a dummy of the magazine's pages showing which ones will contain advertisements and which editorial. (See Figure 6.)

The *art editor* will begin designing some inside pages and the cover and *sub-editors* will start work editing, checking or rewriting any copy which is already on the computer system. They also commission graphics and let the art editor know if a line drawing is required.

The *'furniture' pages* – the standard pages which look the same each month, such as letters and horoscopes – will be designed and edited first and proofs read.

Week two

Weekly conference to discuss progress on the current issue and
forward planning. Writers may be given a new brief, an idea may be
changed or 'spiked', new ideas may be discussed. Decisions will be
made on what will be the main feature at the front of the magazine
and which articles will be prominent.

Work continues on researching and writing features, designing and
editing pages. The fashion department travels abroad for a fashion
shoot. The magazine's columnist provides his copy. The marketing
department briefs the editor on special offers which are planned for
readers.

Week three

Meeting on progress of the issue currently being produced. Second
meeting to make tentative plans for the next issue. About 80 per cent
of the copy and pictures for the current issue is now complete. Copy is
on the computer system, pictures have been scanned.

Final inside pages are designed, followed by the **cover**. The Editor
decides what the 'cover lines' will be (these are the headlines which
appear on the cover and are designed to sell the magazine on the
news-stands).

Sub-editors complete work on all the **inside pages** by the end of
week three, editing the copy and writing the headlines. All
photographs, transparencies and illustrations must now be scanned
onto the production system and the colour checked for accuracy.
Proofs are made as the pages are completed.

Week four

Final **proofs** are made of all pages and checked by department heads.
Changes are made to words and pictures and last minute editing is
done. At this stage, an article can still be dropped and another
substituted if the editor wishes, either because the situation has
changed or for legal reasons.

Week five

Finished pages go to the print site; early copies of the magazine arrive
in the office for final checking. Copies now begin their journey to the
point of sale. Some go overseas, the bulk to newsagents, shops and
kiosks all over Britain. Preview copies go to press and broadcasting
organisations who may use stories or features, thus giving the
magazine free publicity.

Week six

Publication day. Magazine goes on sale.

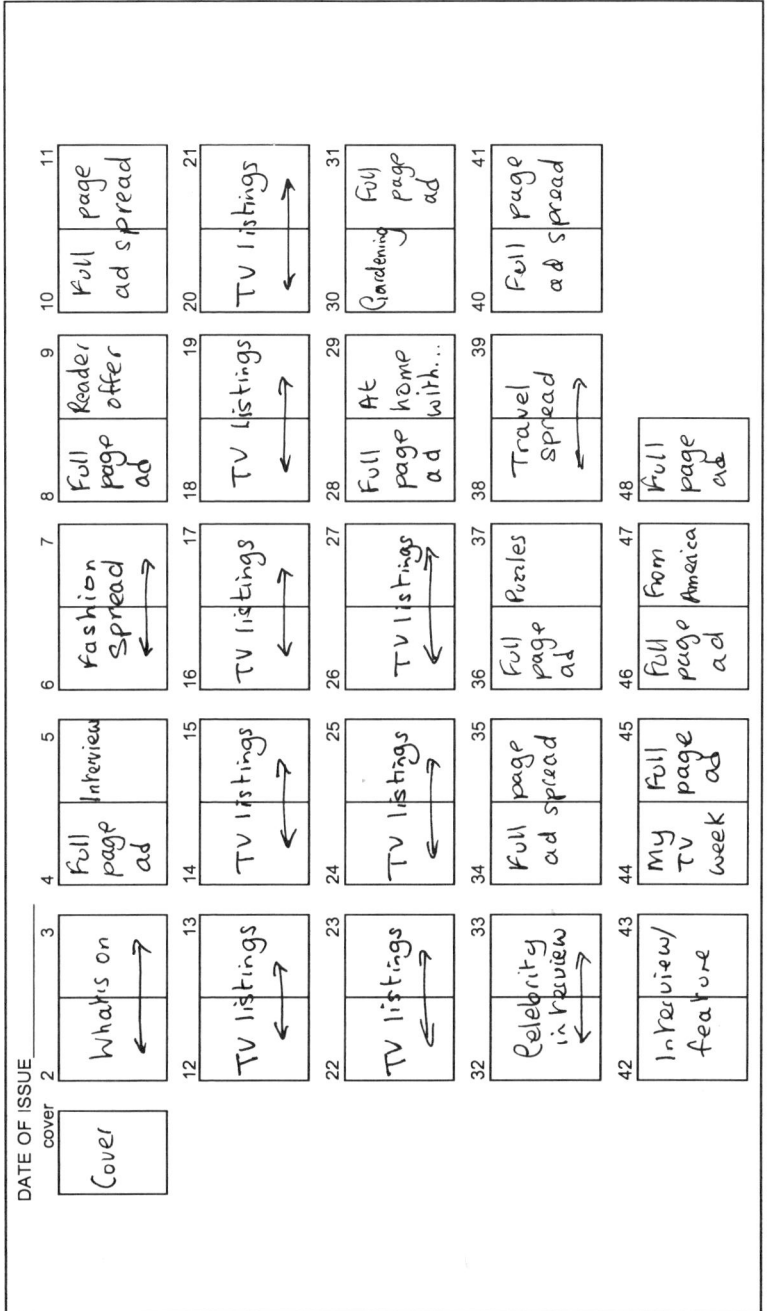

Fig. 6. A magazine flatplan (48-page colour supplement).

SOME JOBS IN MAGAZINES

'The longest lived editor is the one least distinguishable from his average reader.'

Robert Robinson

Editor, listings magazine

This weekly glossy magazine circulates in the capital. It carries a small number of news pages, two or three major features, then theatre, film, television, dance, sport and political listings. The editor supervises a small staff. She commissions features, briefs correspondents, and liaises with the advertising department and the publisher. She oversees the selection of pictures and the design and is responsible for the magazine meeting deadline. She brings her own ideas to the magazine's weekly conference.

In the past month she has:

- Initiated a major investigation into the state of the city's public transport.

- Published a special issue devoted to what the city should do to celebrate the Millennium, encouraging readers to write in with suggestions.

- Organised an award for the city's best restaurants.

A typical day might mean holding a meeting with writers to discuss current projects, visiting the design studio to oversee layout of pages and the cover, meeting the publisher to discuss budgets, meeting the marketing department to discuss promotion of the magazine, reading copy and asking for it to be rewritten, talking by telephone to freelances, selecting photographs for use and, in the evening, attending the première of a play or a film. She might also appear on radio and television news programmes to comment on issues affecting the capital or write features along similar lines for other newspapers and magazines.

You would need considerable experience to apply for this job, probably having started as a writer on a similar magazine and worked your way up.

Writer, house journal

This house journal is a monthly, newsprint newspaper published for the employees of a worldwide banking group. It has only three staff, an editor, a production editor and a staff writer.

The writer must find stories of interest to the readership, research them and write them. He gets ideas for news stories and features from various different sources. One is his contacts in the many different departments of the group, who will tell him when they hear of something of interest.

Changes in the group – reorganisation, new working practices, moving to a new environment – also make stories and features. He reports on staff promotions and interviews people who have recently joined. He might also do a piece on someone who is leaving after a long period, writing about their recollections of changes over the years.

Information issued by the banking group such as profit figures and the annual report will also provide features.

The staff writer also reports on changes and developments outside this group but in the industry – initiatives by other, similar companies, new laws and regulations, government reports.

Some of his recent news stories and features include:

- the group's plans to change bank opening hours
- plans to expand abroad
- new services on offer to customers
- a new scheme for full-time employees to switch to part-time working or job-shares
- an interview with the chief executive about his vision of the banks of the future
- a staff member who raised a large sum for charity on a walk around Britain
- a light-hearted piece on a branch where all the women employees are expecting babies
- an interview with the Banking Ombudsman.

Freelance columnist, current affairs magazine
This is a part-time job and can be combined with other journalistic work or with writing fiction and non-fiction books. The column in question appears monthly in a high-profile, quality magazine. It requires little research but elegant writing; it is opinionated and is written in the first person.

The columnist could write about almost anything from the amusing side of family life to issues of the day. It would take only two or three days a month to do, so is likely to be combined with other work.

This journalist would be a seasoned writer but her or his background would not be important.

Reporter, weekly business magazine

The trade magazine in our example is aimed at people working in advertising and marketing. It contains a mix of news stories and interviews with prominent people in these industries.

This journalist reports news from the advertising agencies – who has won which company's account, staff changes, new agencies setting up – and on magazine and newspaper publishing – the latest circulation figures, new titles, titles closing, the amount spent on advertising and promotion. He might also interview the new head of a thriving advertising agency or the creative director behind a successful ad campaign.

No specialist knowledge would be needed for this job, simply basic reporting skills, a willingness to get to know people in the relevant areas and an ability to hunt out stories.

Sub-editor, newspaper's magazine supplement

This 'magazine' is actually printed on newsprint and given away with the Saturday edition of a quality daily newspaper.

The sub-editor is one of a team of three, supervised by a chief sub and a production editor, all desk bound. Between them, they edit all copy for the magazine, write all the captions for photographs and other illustrations, write the headlines and the cover lines and check page proofs.

They might be working on a major feature in the morning – checking facts and rewriting the copy if necessary – and on a listings section or a recipe page in the afternoon. The sub is responsible for making sure each article reads smoothly, does not leave unanswered questions in the reader's mind, is accurate, is crisply written, and does not contain a libel. The headline must also be accurate and fair yet eye-catching and probably witty. The sub also weighs up the tone of a feature – could it be regarded as offensive or provoke complaints? If in doubt, he will consult the chief sub or editor.

A sub's typical day might be:

- Cutting a major interview with a film celebrity from 3,000 words down to 1,500 and writing the headlines and captions to go with the text.

- Choosing readers' letters and editing them, making sure they are clearly and concisely written and express a point of view.
- Editing a film review from 700 words down to 450.
- Writing the magazine's cover lines.
- Reading and checking proofs of pages which have been subbed by a colleague.

Subs are usually experienced journalists who started out writing, but on some magazines it may be possible to go straight into a subbing post.

Reporter, weekly athletics magazine

This is a glossy magazine with a short lead in time which prides itself on covering as many live events as possible, as well as containing general news and features on athletics.

This reporter will have to travel extensively to cover events on the athletics circuit; in the season he could be at an event in a European city one day and back in Britain, in London or Birmingham, the next.

He will be used to writing fast, because an event may take place only a day before the magazine is due off stone. He will also have a good knowledge of the subject, including its history because he may have to refer to past records, and will have to develop contacts among athletes and promoters.

In one typical week he might have to cover a cross-country event in the north of England, an indoor athletics meeting in Birmingham and a meeting in a European city such as Paris or Rome. In each case he will compile a report of the event and try to get interviews with athletes who featured prominently, possibly breaking a record.

This job would not require any special training; it would be open to any journalist with an extensive knowledge of the subject.

CASE STUDIES

News editor, science journal

Nasreen, 28, left university with a science degree, not really intending to go into journalism until she saw an advertisement for a magazine company's graduate training scheme. She won a place and was taught news and feature writing, interview techniques, law and desktop publishing.

She spent four years with a title published for the food

manufacturing industry before moving to her current magazine, a general science title, as a reporter. She was soon promoted to news editor.

Her **working day** involves co-ordinating copy for the next issue; the magazine is monthly and she is responsible for several news pages. Her work includes:

- Commissioning pieces, deciding whether to use ideas suggested by both staff and freelance writers.

- Briefing writers and, once copy arrives, roughly editing it before passing it to a desk of subs.

- Deciding which stories need illustrations – photographs, graphics or line drawings – and briefing the appropriate departments on what is needed.

- Once copy has been edited, captions and headlines written and illustrations are in place, printing out a proof of the page and checking it again.

She has no plans to move on from her current job at the moment because she enjoys using both her scientific knowledge and her journalistic skills. 'I can't think of any other job that would suit me as well,' she says.

Editor, travel trade magazine

Richard, 30, left school with A-levels in English and Geography. He did a one-year pre-entry course in journalism and was then taken on by a group of weekly newspapers. He continued his training on the job and gained his National Certificate in newspaper journalism.

His overriding interest has always been travel, so he applied for a job as a reporter on this weekly magazine aimed at the travel trade.

For two years he reported on travel fairs at home and abroad and wrote other news stories and features on the travel business. He slowly developed contacts in the large package holiday companies and the airlines.

He covered several exclusive stories, one of which revealed that a well-known package holiday company was on the verge of collapse, while several thousand people were abroad on its pre-paid holidays. After his story appeared, the company was bought out by another group, saving the holidays.

Richard also travelled widely, writing about travel agents, hotels, resorts, airlines, train services and ferries.

At the start of his third year he was appointed deputy editor and two years later editor. He now supervises an editorial staff of nine, writes his own weekly column for the magazine, attends travel industry events and still finds time to visit new resorts and to go on press visits to introduce journalists to new areas of tourism.

In the past year he has reported on:

- A new airline's non-stop flight from London to Sydney.
- The development of a new golf and leisure resort in Spain.
- How an Australian city is building hotels and self-catering villages to house thousands of people during the next Olympic Games.
- An expanding ski area in Canada.

Richard is now using his accumulated knowledge to write a series of travel guides which will be published by his magazine company.

Deputy editor, glossy magazine

Yolanda came into journalism as a late entrant, aged 27, after a career in retail buying. She had always wanted to write and was able to change career when the editor of her local newspaper agreed to give her a six-month trial. Despite her late start she was able to train fully, through block release courses. For several years she stayed with the local weekly, reporting everything from courts and councils to agricultural shows.

She got her first job in national newspapers on one of the Sunday tabloids after selling it a front-page story. She stayed there for six years, quickly becoming one of its prized reporters and getting several exclusives about celebrities and politicians. One revealed the reasons for the breakdown of a Cabinet Minister's marriage.

Then Yolanda was headhunted by a magazine, a glossy 'gossip' title. It wanted to increase its 'newsiness' and put less emphasis on celebrity-led features.

Working with the editor, Yolanda suggests ideas for features and news stories, many of them tips from contacts she has built up during her years in national newspapers. She is also overseeing a redesign of the magazine, to make it look brighter and more immediate. She has introduced a new style of writing for the magazine, encouraging writers to produce sharper, more probing interviews and ask awkward questions.

She no longer writes herself because she does not have time. A typical day involves directing writers, photographers and designers; lunch with a contact; discussions with the editor; reading unedited copy and page proofs.

5

Radio Journalism

'You must get used to travelling around and putting up with unsocial hours, and you must be prepared to talk to anybody about anything – and then sound authoritative immediately afterwards. But it is exciting, challenging – and never dull.'

Tim Smith, BBC local radio trainee

'The interviewee is more important than the presenter. It's the presenter's job to bring out the person because people then speak their minds and listeners identify with them.'

Diana Madill, presenter, *The Magazine*, Radio 5 Live

JOURNALISM PLUS TECHNICAL EXPERTISE PLUS QUICK THINKING

Radio demands all the skills needed in newspapers, and more. As well as finding stories, researching them and interviewing, the radio journalist must have certain technical knowhow. Their job can include reporting live from outside the studio, carrying out studio-based interviews, editing tape and presenting news programmes.

Radio is more immediate than newspapers. As a BBC booklet for potential recruits says: 'Radio is the fastest, most flexible medium for bringing news direct to the public. With a good telephone line you can be on air in seconds.' That means that radio journalists have few second chances. A newspaper reporter may get a chance to rewrite a story before deadline, but radio reporters often have only a few minutes to carry out an interview or script a news story before it is broadcast.

Anyone interested in becoming a radio journalist will obviously need a clear speaking voice as well as the personality to get on with people at all levels, persistence in tracking down a story and excellent knowledge of current affairs at local and national level.

Because news programmes are broadcast live, the ability to work, think and react quickly and meet deadlines is paramount.

THE SCOPE OF RADIO NEWS

Around 90 per cent of the British population listen to radio, according to lecturer and author Michael Bromley (*Teach Yourself Journalism*, 1994).

Radio stations in Britain are either owned by the BBC or by independent companies. Some, such as Reuters Radio which supplies local, national and international news to commercial stations throughout the UK, are part of multi-media groups.

The BBC has five national radio networks, 39 local radio stations, and external services, such as the World Service.

There are also more than 140 independent radio stations. Some broadcast nationally, such as Talk Radio UK, Virgin Radio and Classic FM. Most are regional, such as Capital which broadcasts in London and BRMB in Birmingham.

Not all radio stations carry news programmes, of course; in particular, some regional stations are music-based. But most at least carry bulletins – short summaries of two or three minutes containing the six or seven most important stories of the day.

HOW ARE JOURNALISTS RECRUITED?

Radio journalism is a relatively small branch of the profession. The National Council for the Training of Broadcast Journalists estimated in 1993 that there were only around 5,000 full-time broadcast journalists working in Britain. But broadcasting is likely to expand considerably in the coming decade.

Many journalists moving into radio are already qualified and experienced in print. A large number come from local newspapers. Others join straight from a pre-entry course at college or university, an increasingly common method of entry.

Radio, like other media, employs both staff and freelances. It is also becoming more common, especially in the BBC, for journalists to work on a bi-media basis – that is, for both radio and television. Several of the BBC's foreign and specialist correspondents are bi-media employees.

The opportunities for journalists in radio grew in the 1990s. For example, when Radio 5 launched it was estimated to have created 140 jobs for journalists; when it became Radio 5 Live in 1994 up to another 80 were taken on. Talk Radio UK, the national speech-based commercial station, also took on a number of journalists when it launched in early 1995.

In the future, new technology is likely to bring about the creation of more stations.

THE ROLE OF THE JOURNALIST

'You need to have certain in-built qualities; strong determination to be a journalist, an insatiable thirst for knowledge, a very keen interest in news and current events and the ability to write well.'

A Future in Broadcast Journalism, the National Council for the Training of Broadcast Journalists, 1993

Journalists in radio work on news and current affairs programmes. What is the difference? **News** is typically a report of something that has happened very recently. News can be broadcast in brief summaries, called bulletins, or during longer programmes which may include voice reports and interviews.

Current affairs programmes are usually 30 minutes or more in length, can take the form of documentaries and can investigate or feature one particular issue. They can also include studio discussions or taped interviews.

Both types of radio journalism can include 'actuality' – taped sounds of an event actually happening or other relevant sounds. An example would be the noise of heavy lorries in a piece about a protest over a motorway extension.

Journalists do a multitude of tasks including reporting, interviewing, taping actuality, editing tape, writing scripts and reading them on air, writing and presenting bulletins, and presenting longer programmes. Sometimes they will work with a TO (technical operator), but are increasingly expected to manage the technology as well as the story.

Jobs in radio fall into one of the following categories (see also Figure 7):

Reporter

They travel in the station's broadcast area reporting on events, interviewing, broadcasting live or making taped reports, and interviewing from the studio. They often work alone, with no producer. They also make documentaries or in-depth reports, which are less immediate and usually more analytical.

Specialist correspondent

These are journalists covering a specific area such as law or politics. They track events in their subject and report on them. They can work in either news or current affairs.

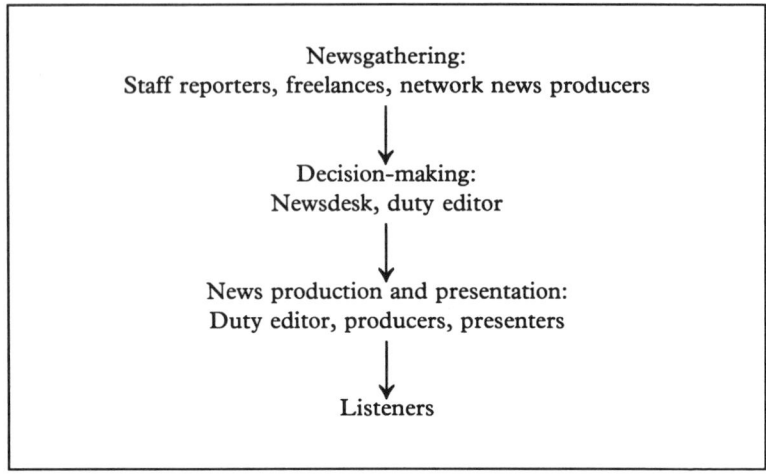

Fig. 7. News flow on a local radio station.

News producer/sub-editor
They compile news bulletins, write scripts to be read on air, fix up interviews for reporters and brief them. They work to tight deadlines, and may read the script as well as writing it. They also work on current affairs programmes, when they decide the style and format, edit tape, write the script or oversee a reporter's script, and approve the finished programme before broadcast.

Programme editor
They direct news producers and reporters, and decide the **running order** of a news bulletin. The running order is the final list showing the order in which headlines and reports will appear, and their duration (see Figure 8).

In current affairs they oversee the making of the programme, deciding how to approach the subject, who to interview and how to edit the film. They also decide the format – for example, whether it will include studio interviews or a panel to answer questions from listeners, or whether it will be a scripted, documentary-style programme.

Presenter
They front current affairs programmes, read continuity announcements and sometimes conduct interviews.

Western Counties Radio

AVON THIS MORNING

RUNNING ORDER

Producer: Davies
Newsdesk: Jones

Guide time	Item	Running time	Elapsed time
0'30"	Avon This Morning jingle	0'30"	0'30"
2'30"	Newsdesk and weather	2'29"	2'59"
2'00"	Music	2'01"	5'00"
2'30"	Intro and billboard 1	2'40"	7'40"
1'30"	Promos	1'17"	8'57"
2'00"	Intro and billboard 2	2'15"	11'12"
2'00"	Music	2'05"	13'17"
2'00"	Intro and billboard 3	2'02"	15'19"
0'30"	Traffic reports	0'29"	15'48"
1'00"	Newsdesk	1'00"	16'48"
2'00"	Intro and billboard 4	2'01"	18'49"
2'30"	Music	2'30"	21'19"
4'00"	Sportsdesk	3'50"	25'09"
1'30"	Newsdesk	1'25"	26'34"
2'30"	Intro and billboard 5	2'25"	28'59"
1'00"	Closing newsdesk	1'01"	30'00"
Outro			

This is the running order for a 30-minute morning news and music programme. Western Counties Radio works to a standard format. The column on the left shows how much time should be allocated to each item. The central column describes the item – music or talk – and the column on the right shows the actual running time.

Fig. 8. Radio running order.

Newsreader

They read news bulletins and often write them as well, in consultation with a programme editor. They may also do live interviews.

Many journalists combine the roles of presenter and newsreader, or are both producers and presenters or reporters and newsreaders.

TYPICAL RADIO JOBS

Here is a more detailed look at some typical jobs in radio:

Producer/presenter, BBC local radio station in the West Country

This journalist has wide experience in newspapers and radio. The job covers hosting live phone-in programmes, carrying out live and recorded interviews, chairing debates, presenting documentaries and originating ideas.

The producer/presenter is involved in making her programmes from the original idea through to the finished tape.

Her essential qualities are a charismatic personality capable of gaining the loyalty of listeners, good voice delivery and the ability to communicate well with people from all walks of life. She also has to be able to react quickly during live broadcasts and remain calm and collected in dealing with vociferous interviewees and unruly listeners on the phone.

She needs a good knowledge of production techniques and the ability to do outside broadcasts as well as work from a studio. The mainstay of the job is a three-hour weekday show, broadcast in mid-morning. The show contains a phone-in section, a live interview on a topical issue, a studio debate, news bulletins and special reports.

Producer, network radio religious programme

This producer is responsible for shaping the programme. He has experience of journalism and of live radio, and a wide knowledge of religious and ethical issues.

Daily tasks include originating ideas for news stories and features on religious topics, commissioning material from staff and free-lances and discussing stories with reporters, presenters and other producers.

In consultation with the programme editor, the producer determines the running order of the items for each weekly programme, deciding the length and priority of each. He oversees interviews, directing the reporter's questions if necessary, and the editing of pre-recorded material.

Bi-media foreign correspondent, BBC

This correspondent is an experienced journalist with a background in radio news reporting. His bi-media role means he has had to learn television techniques as well. He has to have a broad knowledge of the culture and demography of the area to which he has been posted, and fluency in the language.

The correspondent travels extensively throughout the country or region, reporting for both radio and television on the political, economic and social issues of the area. Reports have to be made interesting to a British audience.

Day-to-day work could be:

- filing a live report on a riot or demonstration for the mid-evening television news
- making a radio documentary on poverty in the country's capital city
- reporting on an election campaign for both media
- interviewing a politician accused of a scandal for world service broadcasting.

The correspondent is used to working alone or with a sound or camera crew, is technically competent, and able to come up with plenty of ideas for news stories and features.

Freelance radio sports correspondent

The prerequisites for this job are a good knowledge of the sports to be covered, a good broadcasting manner, a clear voice and the ability to stay calm under pressure.

This correspondent works alone, offering reports and interviews to several different radio stations, including Radio 5 Live and local outlets.

He covers evening and weekend football matches in his area, reporting live for either network or local radio. He travels frequently to away games of local teams. He also covers rugby and, less often, boxing. He has a large network of contacts within these sports and often interviews players and managers after a match.

His radio work takes up only two or two and a half days a week, so he also works for local and national newspapers and for sports magazines. He is sometimes able to report live for radio, write a news story for a national newspaper and a feature for a magazine from the same event. His work is in fairly short, intensive bursts – he is extremely busy when a match is being played and just afterwards, then may have a couple of days when little is happening.

To make sure he does not waste time or work, he negotiates with the sports editor of either a radio station or a newspaper before covering an event, so that his work is 'commissioned'.

Duty editor, radio news network providing bulletins to commercial stations

This is a job for an experienced radio journalist. The duty editor, working on a shift pattern, oversees a team of journalists producing bulletins 24 hours a day. An extra responsibility involves organising shift patterns to provide 24-hour coverage.

She works at the heart of the newsroom, directing reporters about which stories they should cover and the approach they should take. She also briefs producers who then write scripts and edit tape.

The duty editor decides the running order for bulletins, allocates a given amount of time for each story, and decides whether voice reports or live interviews will be used. She then reads the finished script for a bulletin, and, if there is time, may alter or rewrite it.

She is responsible for making sure bulletins are fair, accurate and legal, and that all the relevant stories of the day have been covered.

INSIDE THE NEWSROOM

'Programming has traditionally not been as important an issue for radio as it has been for the UK's television channels. Yes, Radio 4 has programmes in that each feature's content is different from another's. Elsewhere in radio, such differences tend not to exist, with the station format, be it news or music, permeating every programme and the presenter adding the twist.'

Alec Kenny, sales director Talk Radio UK
(*Media Week*)

Radio newsrooms are as varied as the stories they report. Some work 24 hours day, like London News Radio in the capital; others wind down in the early evening. But their working methods are similar.

Radio newsrooms are divided into **input** and **output**. At the heart of input is the newsdesk, led by a news editor. Here stories flow in from different sources, such as agency reports, the station's own journalists, the emergency services, news conferences and press releases and other media (for example, local newspapers).

The output is controlled by a station editor or programme editor. He or she leads a team of producers who package the input into bulletins and programmes for transmission.

Input: where stories come from

Like newspapers, radio newsrooms centre on a diary of events to be covered which will provide stories and features. Reporters will also cover off-diary and unexpected events, such as the sudden resignation of the manager of the local football team.

Radio reporters are encouraged to be investigative, working on tips from contacts to track down exclusive stories. They are expected to find human interest stories, originate ideas for documentaries and follow them through, identify local issues which can be debated on air and find controversial or interesting people to feature in programmes. They will also have to report breaking news stories quickly, accurately and fairly, even something that is happening as a news bulletin is broadcast.

The areas of responsibility for radio journalists are fluid and they can expect to do more than one job. A reporter may get a chance to do some presenting or producing; a producer may sometimes read a news bulletin; a presenter may go on the road to do an outside broadcast; a sub-editor could become involved in making a documentary.

Some independent stations' staff is so small that one journalist may have to report, present and produce for the same programme. The BBC particularly encourages journalists to become multi-skilled, to the point where it has proposed that its radio journalists should carry camcorders so they can film reports for television before a traditional camera crew arrives. Union opposition has so far stopped this becoming common practice, but broadcast journalists are certainly likely to find themselves carrying out a wide range of tasks.

The news schedule

As an example, we will look at a fictional BBC station, Western Counties Radio. It covers a large area in the West Country. Below is its news schedule for one typical day. The schedule is the basis for the first news conference of the day, at 9am. The main news programmes are at one 1pm and 5pm with half-hourly bulletins in between. Each item begins with the name of the reporter covering.

WESTERN COUNTIES RADIO
Newsgathering prospects Fri 10 May 199X
Local

News editor: Hargreaves
Reporters: Stevens, Peters, Sitaram, Jones, Angel, Morrison
Presenting: Baptiste

Local elections Liberal Democrats are celebrating sweeping gains in district and both county councils. Tories left with almost no seats, Labour results poor.
STEVENS: main package for one o'clock and five o'clock. Results, ints with all three party leaders. 10.30am: Tory news conf County Hall; 11am Lib Dem news conf at HQ (radio car); 11.30am Labour news conf Civic Centre.
PETERS: vox pops from Dursley estate and High Green village for one o'clock.
Farmers' scare Sitaram: Report in *Lancet* says sheep dip causing long-term medical problems and disability. Ints local farmers and NFU spokesman for one o'clock.
Inquest Morrison: Into death of aristocrat's daughter living in bedsit, drugs suspected. Council chamber, 11am. Pre-recorded int with brother. Verdict for five o'clock.
Neighbourhood watch initiative Macintyre: Launch of new police initiative for more neighbourhood watch groups. County police HQ, 12 noon.
Unfair sacking claim Jones: Sacked office worker is suing her former employer, managing director of electronics business, claiming sexual harassment. Ind trib. Civic Centre: 11am. Decision likely for five o'clock.
Theatre Sitaram: New production at Wyvern Theatre. Press call, 5pm. Ints with director/cast.
Celebrity wedding Angel: Pop star expected to marry at village church, Downend. 3.30pm (tip-off). (Radio car.)
Also watching
- Possible resignation of housing committee chairman. Follows row over allegations of homes for votes.
- Meadowhall estate: all quiet after yob violence but keeping watch.

As well as covering stories on its own patch, Western Counties Radio will take national and international stories from network radio news. It will also provide stories for the network.

Off-diary stories

There will also be many off-diary stories to be reported. How does the newsdesk find out about these?

Members of the public may phone in, reporters may be tipped off by their contacts, a statement may be issued and faxed to the newsroom, they may be discovered during a check call to the emergency services, or they may be reported in other media. These are called 'breaking' stories. Reporters working on a diary story may have to put that on hold and cover a more important breaking story. The immediate steps are to:

- Contact someone for information.
- Go to the scene.
- Find witnesses to interview.

As an example, let's take a motorway crash. The reporter finds out about the story when a member of the public phones in at 10.45am to say she can see the crash. She has heard the wail of emergency sirens and, from a back window of her house, can just glimpse cars and what she describes as 'lots of people milling about.'

- The reporter gets the location from her and sets off for the scene.

- Meanwhile, another reporter calls the emergency services to confirm what has happened. That gives enough information for a headline on the 11am bulletin.

- The reporter gets as near to the scene as she can. She interviews police who have cordoned off the carriageway and manages to find several drivers and passengers who have walked away unscathed.

- Meanwhile a reporter back in the newsroom presses police headquarters for an official estimate of dead and injured.

- A fuller story can be pieced together for the one o'clock news. It includes a live voice report from the journalist at the scene, and interviews with people she has spoken to.

- By the five o'clock news, there is substantially more information. Police have said how many are dead and injured and identified the cause of the crash – one car with a burst tyre.

- One reporter, working from the studio, has taped an interview with a senior police officer. Police have also given a phone number for worried members of the public.

- A radio car has joined the reporter at the scene, giving her the ability to broadcast live, studio-quality interviews with police, witnesses and survivors.

Radio is at the forefront of reporting breaking stories. Newspapers must obviously wait for their normal deadlines. Television can broadcast a newsflash or a presenter reading a headline with a taped voice report from the scene, but is obviously hampered by lack of 'visuals'.

Output: a mix of stories

Radio news programmes will carry a mix of local, national and international news, not necessarily in that order. The programme editor or news producer will decide which is the most important story of the day. It could be a national one – for example, a speech by the Prime Minister on the economy – or a local one, perhaps a company announcing redundancies or a violent crime on the streets of a town in the area.

Different stations have different policies. Some prefer to lead on a local story, following with more local material and winding up with the national headlines. Others will judge stories on their strength, regardless of where they originated. Some include foreign stories, others do not. Policy is usually set by the Head of News.

Some local stations take bulletins from a network provider, such as IRN or Reuters Radio. These concentrate on national and foreign news, but the station may add its own local headlines. They may also use part of the network bulletin, combining it with their own material.

Bulletins on network radio, such as Radio 4 or Radio 5 Live, will contain national and international news.

Planning the programme: running order

The programme editor is the key figure in deciding what will be output. He or she works out the running order of a news programme. First, he or she will consult the news schedule to see what stories are being covered, and what 'packages' are available. A package is a tape including a combination of voice reports, interviews and actuality.

The programme editor will rate the stories available in order of importance and decide how much time to give to each. The running order can change frequently as new stories develop, right up until the last seconds before transmission. Even as a bulletin is going out, the order can be changed and new scripts substituted for old.

This could be the running order for a four-minute bulletin, based on the news schedule above and including breaking stories:

Motorway crash – 2.00 (two minutes)
Local elections – 0.45
Unfair sacking – 0.15
Inquest verdict – 0.15
Celebrity wedding – 0.15
Promo (trailer for later news programmes) – 0.10
Sport and weather – 0.20

How are news items chosen?

Selecting news items takes practice and experience. Many journalists say it becomes instinctive, but that in the early days they made a lot of wrong decisions.

The programme editor must be familiar with the tastes and demands of the station's audience. For example, is it primarily a farming community, who would want to hear news about agriculture? Is it a commuter belt, with an interest in financial news? Is the audience mainly male or female, young or elderly? Every radio station will know the **profile** of its listeners, and what they are interested in. To some extent, that profile will dictate what sort of news is covered.

The programme editor will also evaluate each story, asking:

- Is this story of interest locally?
- Does it affect people here?
- If it is a national story, is it significant enough to go higher in the running order than local stories?
- Do we have voice reports and interviews to break up the scripted broadcast?
- Can we get the tape back to the studio on time, or can we do an outside broadcast? (An outside broadcast is one done from the scene of an event, by telephone or radio car.)

Making it fit

Whether the news programme in question is three minutes or thirty minutes long, it must be timed exactly. There is no leeway for it to overrun, even by two or three seconds.

How is this done? The news presenter in the studio is responsible for keeping exactly to the times allowed in the running order. As many reports as possible are scripted, so that they are exactly the right length. Reporters who are going to come into the programme live are warned how long they will be on air.

Broadcast journalists allow three words per second, so a one-minute report would be 180 words, a 30-second taped interview would have 90 words, and so on.

Current affairs programmes

Radio journalists do not work only on news programmes, but also in current affairs. The programmes can be:

- *Documentaries/investigations* – taped reports including interviews.

- *Talk programmes* – discussion programmes, either with guests in a studio or with callers phoning in.

Some of those broadcasting nationally in 1996 were *The Magazine* on Radio 5 Live, *Today in Parliament* on Radio 4, *Woman's Hour*, also on Radio 4, and *Ruscoe on Five* (Radio 5 Live).

Our fictional BBC station, Western Counties Radio, broadcasts a nightly current affairs programme called *The West Tonight*. It includes debate about and analysis of recent news events, using live and taped interviews. It also has a slot for a lengthy feature on a matter of local interest. Some possible subjects would be:

- How church attendances have fallen. A reporter interviewed local churchmen/women and did a vox pop of residents. (A **vox pop** is simply a series of short interviews, carried out in the street. Interviewees are picked at random.)

- An interview with a local author who has just published a new novel. The reporter asked her questions about the book and about her life in the area.

- A day with the local fire brigade. A reporter spent a shift with one fire team, using actuality, interviews and voice reports to convey the drama and danger in the life of local firemen.

A hectic lifestyle

Radio journalists work on several projects at once, organising interviews and recording material for feature programmes in between writing and broadcasting news stories. Like newspaper journalists, they work long hours and are usually on a rota including nights and weekends.

Below is a typical week's news and current affairs programming at our fictional Western Counties Radio. The station also schedules music and arts programmes. News bulletins go out on the half hour or the hour, depending on the time of day. They can be three, four or five minutes long.

A week of programming at Western Counties Radio
Weekdays

6am-9.30am News magazine programme of bulletins, travel and longer reports on local issues and personalities. The programme has a high news content and contains broadcasts from in the studio and outside.

12.30pm-1pm Lunchtime magazine programme looks behind the news, getting reaction to the stories of the day and analysis of the events. Studio based, it has a high content of interviews from those involved in local stories. News headlines complete the programme.

4.30pm-6pm 'PM' news magazine. A full round-up of the day's local, national and international news, with one special in-depth report and one studio interview. The aim is to give listeners detailed, expanded news coverage.

Saturday

Three-minute news bulletins throughout the morning, on the hour or half hour.

7am-10.30am – Magazine programme including news and travel. Discussion by guests in the studio of controversial local issues, lifestyle and leisure features, such as a short 'gardeners' questions' and reviews of current concerts, film and theatre in the region.

The emphasis is less on hard news – although the headlines are repeated on the hour – and more on entertainment, the arts and weekend pursuits. There might be a feature about a threatened nature reserve, an interview with a rock star performing locally, or a report on new sports facilities in the area.

2pm-6pm Saturday sport – reports of local events. Staff reporters or freelances will cover football, rugby and any other major sports events in the area live. There will be studio discussion of the matches and results.

Sunday

Three-minute news bulletins go out on the hour from 8am until 1pm.

12 noon A 'this week' magazine programme goes behind the headlines about recent events in the area. There will be reports by journalists who have covered big stories during the week. It will also review the Sunday papers.

RADIO TECHNIQUES: HOW A STORY GETS ON AIR

'Everything that can be said can be said clearly.'
                                        Ludwig Wittgenstein

Radio journalists need extra skills. They must know how to write scripts, read the news, ,interview on air and operate their own equipment.

Writing scripts: talking to the listener

New recruits quickly learn that writing for radio – and television – is different from writing for print. Broadcast journalists must write 'conversationally', which means as if they were holding a one-to-one conversation with another person (see Figure 9).

A bulletin written in newspaper style would sound formal and stilted if read out on air. A radio listener's attention span is, on average, three minutes, so every word must count.

Writing conversationally is one of the most important skills for a radio journalist, and is well worth mastering before applying for jobs or college courses. How is it done?

- Pretend you are actually speaking – talk into the keyboard.
- Use clear, concise, plain English.
- Be concrete and positive.
- Avoid formal language, jargon and clichés.
- Make it interesting and entertaining.
- Use contractions, such as 'that's', rather than two words, such as 'that is'.
- Keep to sentences of 25 words or less.
- Avoid tongue-twisters and unintentional rhymes.
- Have a strong ending.
- Always read your script aloud beforehand.

Newsreading: some tips

Newsreading takes practice, but here are some pointers.

- The standard speed is 180 words per minute, so read aloud until you are familiar with the pace.
- Learn to control your breathing – you must not run out of breath at the wrong moment.
- Emphasise key words in the script – for example: 'News just in. *Four people* are believed to have *died* when a *fishing boat* sank off the coast near *Whitehaven* this afternoon.'

Western Counties Radio

NEWS CUE SHEET

Title: blaze

Date: 20.4   **Time**: 11.20

Words: JT   **Audio**: PM

For broadcast: today **Bulletin(s)**: 12noon, 1pm, 4pm, 6pm

Credit:

Copy taken by:

A huge FIRE has today swept through a 12-storey OFFICE building in the centre of Bristol. At least a DOZEN people have been taken to hospital suffering the effects of smoke. Up to TEN local BUSINESSES have been disrupted.
Fireman brought the blaze under control in the past few minutes. It's believed to have started on the SIXTH FLOOR but the cause isn't yet known.
Our reporter Peter Mannion is at the scene...

Cut: blaze **Dur**: 21 **Out**:....Mannion, Parkway, Bristol **Tot**: 60

The news cue sheet is the scripted intro to a news story. It shows the title of the story, the date and time it was prepared, the initials of the producer in the studio and the reporter at the scene. It also shows which bulletins it is expected to go out on. In this case it is to be followed by a taped or live voice report. At the end it shows the duration of the script and the voice report that follows it and the 'out' words of the voice report.

Fig. 9. A radio script.

- Beware of other sounds – for example, turning over sheets of paper.
- Try to sound as though you are talking to someone, not reading aloud.
- Check the pronunciation of names and places before you go on air.
- Don't eat or drink minutes before you begin and have a glass of water beside you.

Interviewing on air: telling a story

Interviews are intended to get other people to talk, so that you can broadcast their version of events. Questions have to be carefully phrased to achieve this. You do not want a tape where you ask a long question, and the interviewee replies: 'Yes' or 'No'. You want them to tell the story in their own words.

For example, you are interviewing police about the disappearance of a teenage girl. Here are two different ways you could begin your question-and-answer session on tape.

1. *You*: 'Is it correct that Lisa was last seen at eight o'clock this morning?'
   Police officer: 'That's right.'

2. *You*: 'Can you give me some details about when Lisa was seen last?'
   Police officer: 'Yes. It was eight o'clock this morning. She set off for school exactly as usual. She had her school bag with her, a large rucksack, and she said goodbye to her mum and dad quite cheerfully...'

Interviews can adopt different styles. They can be:

- **Confrontational**, in which the reporter challenges the interviewee. This is used in investigative reporting.
- **Emotional**, in which you lead someone to tell a dramatic or sad story in their own words.
- **Informational**, where the reporter tries to elicit facts.

CASE STUDIES

Presenter, network radio magazine show

James, 35, graduated with a degree in geography and travelled around the world for two years. On his return he applied to television stations for reporting jobs. He feels he was extremely lucky to land a post as a television reporter for the BBC in Scotland.

After four years he switched to reporting and presenting for a prestigious morning radio news and current affairs programme. He says that this was where he really became hooked on working in radio and that he learned a lot from the programme's seasoned professionals.

After another three years he felt he wanted a change. A new network was launching, and he let it be known he was interested. James was then approached to present a mid-morning magazine programme.

Now he does everything from chairing a studio discussion to hosting a phone-in, as well as delivering hard news and carrying out interviews when necessary. James works closely with the programme editor in deciding topics for discussions and phone-ins, and the format of the programme.

He particularly enjoys being able to combine news presenting and interviewing with hosting live debates and also with talking to members of the public, and making it possible for them to have their say on air.

He says he simply loves radio. 'When I was travelling after university, my constant companion was the World Service. I've listened to the radio most of my waking hours since then.'

Freelance medical journalist

After gaining a science degree, Karen began her career working on a trade magazine for GPs. She worked her way up the career ladder and was appointed deputy editor of the magazine after five years. As well as writing for the magazine, commissioning articles, overseeing production and forward planning, she began to be asked to contribute to radio news and current affairs programmes because of her specialist knowledge on health and medical matters.

When she married and had children, Karen decided she did not want to work full-time. After leaving the magazine she planned to write only several features a month, spending the rest of her time with her children. The calls from radio stations, however, continued, and she discovered that she enjoyed this aspect of her freelance career hugely.

During the next few years she became a familiar voice on local radio, taking part in debates and often being interviewed about developments concerning the health service, doctors, the nursing profession and other medical matters. She was soon offered her own weekly programme, *Health Matters*, at her local station. The second series was syndicated to several other stations.

As well as coming up with ideas for the programme, reporting and presenting it, Karen, now 37, has done one-off programmes, such as a documentary on a measles epidemic and an investigation into the treatment of AIDS patients in the area.

Now that her children are at school, Karen is preparing to make more one-off programmes but wants to continue working as a freelance so that her hours are flexible. She also plans to try her hand at making television documentaries, and is currently undertaking a short course in TV reporting and presentation in preparation. 'The best thing about my work is being able to choose how much I do, and when,' she says.

6

Inside Television News

'A constant criticism of TV's political coverage is that complex issues are squeezed into soundbites – the equivalent of forcing a Sunday lunch of roast beef and two veg into a burger bun. But soundbites are the preserve of TV news, while (Sunday) interview programmes offer a Chinese banquet for journalists... a Cabinet Minister interviewed live on TV cannot declare his opposition to the single currency but then subsequently ask not to be identified.'

Alastair Stewart, presenter of GMTV's
The Sunday Programme (writing in *The Guardian*)

'British broadcasting, in all its manifestations, has earned from its audiences a trust and credibility that no longer attaches to many newspapers.'

Michael Grade, former chief executive of Channel 4
(*New Statesman*)

BRINGING THE NEWS TO A HUGE AUDIENCE

Television journalists have an audience which any actor or showbusiness personality would envy. Tens of millions of people tune in to news bulletins and current affairs programmes each day. For example:

- 6.6 million viewers watch *News At Ten.*
- 5.7 million tune in to the BBC's *Nine O'Clock News.*
- 6.3 million for the *Six O'Clock News.*
- 4.9 million switch on for ITN's *Early Evening News* at 5.45pm.
- The BBC's lunchtime news attracts an audience of 3.4 million.
- ITN's rival programme has 2.5 million.

One survey showed that around 80 per cent of the population use television as their main source of news, as compared to 25 per cent who cite a daily newspaper.

Television news channels are proliferating. Channel 5 launched a 24-hour service with several bulletins a day and over 100 journalists in 1997. The BBC decided to expand WSTV (world service television) into Europe with a team of 110 journalists working in its newsroom and is considering the USA, Australasia and South America.

Digital broadcasting, due in the next few years, is likely to open the airwaves to many more channels.

The job: no two days are the same

Journalists in television may work on news or magazine programmes, or both. An example of a news programme is ITV's *News At Ten*, and a current affairs programme could be BBC's *Panorama*. Journalists may end up producing the 'soundbites' that Alastair Stewart refers to, or doing an in-depth interview with a politician; they may work on a two-minute news report or an hour-long documentary.

As in radio, reporters and correspondents will do outside broadcasts, studio interviews and write their own scripts; editors and producers will be desk-based and will write 'intros' to scripts, supervise videotape editing, and direct reporters. A television journalist may work in Britain or abroad and travel frequently. Their work is extremely varied.

For example, here are three very different days in the life of one TV reporter:

- *Day one*: a sensitive interview with a family who are suing a hospital for compensation after their young son died during an operation. Travel to family's home in Scotland to videotape interview, then to hospital in nearby town.

- *Day two*: reporting on the annual meeting of a large company whose shareholders have expressed 'no confidence' in the chairman. Central London.

- *Day three*: travel to the north of the country to report on the havoc caused by freak, heavy rain which has left cities under water.

A journalist working on a weekly current affairs programme would spend several days or longer on one subject. The subjects for current affairs are infinite – anything from a single currency for Europe to the number of single parents supported by state benefits.

Current affairs programmes take many forms. For example, they can be interview-based, such as BBC's *Breakfast With Frost*, or investigation-based, such as ITV's *World In Action*.

Television journalism is no less dangerous than working for newspapers. TV correspondents may be sent to a war zone or to cover a riot. One example was the former BBC television correspondent Martin Bell, caught in crossfire in Bosnia. As the BBC states in its booklet, *The Way In: Job Opportunities*: 'Working conditions are often uncomfortable at best.'

What qualities does a TV journalist need?

Television reporters, like those on newspapers, need persistence, good general knowledge, an excellent grasp of current affairs, the ability to think quickly and marshal facts logically and the talent of getting on with all sorts of people.

One of the most important attributes is to be able to **remain calm and cool** in the face of strict deadlines or unscripted disasters. Like radio journalists, they must often report live. They may arrive at an incident just a few minutes before their report is due on air. They must assess the situation quickly, get whatever facts they can, find people to interview and be ready to face the camera shortly afterwards, sounding authoritative and providing an accurate summary of events.

Television journalists working in the newsroom face similar strict deadlines. They may have to write a script for a news bulletin as an event is still happening, being fed information from reporters at the scene. The BBC tells potential recruits they will almost certainly be 'preparing one story while the previous one is on air.'

Those working on current affairs or news magazine programmes often have much less demanding deadlines and are able to investigate the subject for a programme thoroughly.

All TV journalists must be able to work on their own initiative, but also as part of a team. Usually they will be accompanied by a technical crew. This can be an 'OMB' (one man band) or a camera operator and sound and lighting technicians.

A new breed of **'videojournalists'**, such as those working for cable companies like Channel One in London, operate their own equipment, carrying a camcorder on their shoulders while out reporting and conducting interviews.

Getting into TV

Journalists applying to become television news **trainees** will need exceptional educational qualifications. Competition for traineeships in television news is fierce and standards are high. 'The highly motivated and the very highly motivated' was how the candidates on the final shortlist for graduate traineeships with the BBC in 1994 were described. The remark was made by Samir Shah, head of political programmes for BBC News and Current Affairs (*The Times*). He added that the final 24 candidates were distinguished by having 'independence of thought' and being 'confident, articulate and assured'.

Eight were taken on. Of them, six were Oxbridge graduates in arts subjects, three of whom had been educated at comprehensive or grammar schools; the others were from UMIST (University of Manchester Institute of Science and Technology) and Bristol University. Shah concluded: 'It has to be said that in this case, Oxbridge still delivered.'

You will not need an Oxbridge degree for every job in television news or current affairs, but remember that it is one of the most competitive areas of journalism.

Many journalists entering television are qualified and have already worked in radio. They then apply for **specific job vacancies** rather than traineeships, but the competition is still tough.

Researchers and technical staff such as videotape editors are sometimes able to retrain as television reporters or news producers.

Where are the jobs?
The opportunities in television journalism are growing as more channels – terrestrial, satellite and cable – open up. The BBC employs thousands of journalists on its domestic services and World Service Television. Many more work for other organisations such as ITN (Independent Television News), the regional newsrooms of the independent television companies, Sky News, Reuters Television and small cable news stations such as Channel One and Live TV in the capital.

British journalists, such as Brent Sadler, are sometimes taken on by CNN, the American news channel which broadcasts worldwide. Anyone with an interest in sport could apply to Sky's sports channels or to Eurosport, and it seems likely that many more sports channels will be launched when the switch is made to digital broadcasting.

What kind of jobs are there?
Jobs fall into similar categories to those in radio, but vary from station to station (see also Figure 10).

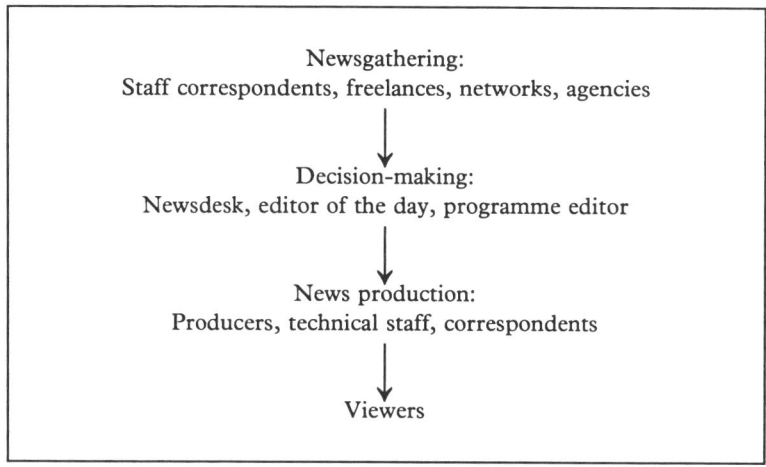

Fig. 10. News flow on a regional television station.

- **Reporters** go out of the office on news stories, both diary and off-diary. They find out as much as possible about the background to the story, go to the scene and carry out interviews. They may interview on camera, report from the location, or return to the studio and write a script for a news bulletin. They can be asked to report on almost any event taking place in Britain or abroad.

  Here are some examples of television news stories which would be covered by general reporters:

  1. A new report says London is the most litter-strewn capital in Europe. A reporter and camera crew go out to find examples of London's litter problem and interview people working and living in the capital. They also talk to environmental health officials.

  2. A baby is kidnapped from a provincial hospital. A reporter from ITN, BBC or a local television newsroom goes to the hospital, interviews parents and hospital officials and attends a news conference.

  3. An awards ceremony for the acting profession. A reporter and camera crew attend the ceremony, get interviews with winners and reaction from their contemporaries. Back in the studio, the live report has scenes from an award-winning film cut in.

- **Correspondents** are specialists, often working on a bi-media basis, who have their own subjects to cover – health, environment, the law, the economy, politics, religious affairs, crime and so on. Examples include:

1. An *environment* correspondent reports on a serious pollution incident affecting a river or the coast.

2. A *legal* correspondent reports on government proposals for a change in the law, and analyses the importance of a test case in the High Court.

3. A *health* correspondent investigates and presents a report on a measles epidemic affecting children throughout Britain.

- **Foreign correspondents** are based by television companies in major cities such as Washington or Paris; they often cover the country for radio and television.

- **News editors** direct reporters, telling them which stories they will work on, who to approach for information and how long a report is likely to be. They also discuss correspondents' stories with them and will compile a schedule of the news items that are being worked on for the various conferences held throughout the day.

- **Programme editors** decide which stories will be included in a bulletin and direct the news editor. They also decide which story will be the lead item, the length of other reports and what will be scripted or live. Major news bulletins, such as the BBC's *Nine O'Clock News*, have their own editor. In a regional television station, an editor may work on several bulletins throughout the day.

- **Producers** help compile bulletins, writing intros to scripts, supervising videotape editing, commissioning graphics and setting up interviews for reporters.

- **Presenters** introduce programmes, reading scripts and bulletins and sometimes interviewing. Appearance and voice are important if you want to become a presenter, but most are experienced journalists too. A solid background in television news equips them to cope with the unforeseen, such as the breakdown of a live report or the failure of a satellite link.

In common with other media, there is a trend in television towards **multi-skilling**, with journalists doing more than one specific task.

PROGRAMMING: NEWS AND CURRENT AFFAIRS

'Rolling news is a hungry beast. As soon as you've fed it, it wants more.'

Nick Pollard, programme chief, Channel One
(*ES Magazine, Evening Standard*)

'It (*Panorama*) must be a strong narrative programme. It is long form journalism, more like a newspaper's news feature which must have a strong start, middle and end. It is not a documentary, but has the documentary elements of telling a story.'

Tim Gardam, editor of BBC weekly current affairs programmes (writing in *The Guardian*, 1995)

News and current affairs programmes deal with similar subjects but their treatment of it is different.

Characteristics of news
- Reports are short, as little as one minute.
- Reporters and correspondents may report live, without editing.
- There will be a large number of items in each bulletin.
- Many different journalists will contribute to each bulletin.
- Events reported are recent and may still be happening.
- Reports are factual, unbiased and aim to inform viewers as fully as possible in the time available.
- Deadlines are strict, and short.

Characteristics of current affairs
- Lengthier than news, typically half an hour or 50 minutes.
- Programmes are pre-recorded and edited.
- They are predominantly single subject.
- Issues covered are topical, but programmes may analyse as well as state facts.
- A programme may be made over several weeks, allowing greater time for research.
- Programmes are made by small teams, usually with only one on-screen reporter/presenter.

What goes into a news bulletin?
The programme editor must use the important stories of the day, but he or she will also try to get a balance of items. There will be

some home news, some foreign; home news will be national and local; most of it will be serious but this will be balanced with a light-hearted item near the end of the programme.

There will also be a mixture of headlines, intros and scripts read live from the studio, newly recorded videotape, library tape, still photographs, graphics, recorded interviews and live reports and interviews. The launch of Channel 5 has introduced an alternative presentation for television news. To appeal to a younger audience the format is less formal, with presenters roaming the studio delivering bulletins in a chatty style. BBC, ITV and Sky have chosen to retain a traditional format.

These were the stories broadcast by BBC's *Six O'Clock News* on a Thursday evening in early 1995:

The programme opened with four main headlines.
1. French seamen blockade Calais in a protest against a British ferry company, leaving thousands of people stranded.
2. An inquiry reveals that George Graham, the sacked manager of Arsenal Football Club, received £400,000 in transfer commissions.
3. New rules proposed by the government would mean more old people having to pay for care in private nursing homes.
4. British Gas announced profits of £1.25 billion, provoking an outcry from the Opposition.

The newsreader returned to the Calais story
He read a script outlining the reasons for the dispute as current videotape of the port and traffic chaos in the town was shown. There was a recorded interview with the seamen's leader and others with stranded travellers. The item finished with the newsreader interviewing the reporter at the scene live.

Next came the Arsenal item
The newsreader read an intro to videotape of a news conference held by football's governing body, the Premier League. Library tape of George Graham signing autographs and of one transferred player accompanied the script.

The report also showed Premier League and Football Association executives making statements and ended with the reporter on camera, summarising the developments.

The health care item was presented by a social affairs correspondent
There was a case study – one woman affected – and an interview with her husband. The script gave general information on the number of hospital beds for old people to library tape of a hospital.

Details of the new guidelines were repeated in a graphic. There was a recorded interview with the head of a charity and a statement taped in the studio by a junior health minister.

The bulletin contained several other stories
Each got between 45 seconds and two and a half minutes. Some were little more than headlines read by the newsreaders. Sometimes videotape was shown. Other items were more detailed with taped interviews.

There was little live reporting from correspondents
Other stories included:

1. British Gas profits, with tape of the Opposition leader, Tony Blair, in the Commons that afternoon.
2. Four men to appear at Belfast Crown Court to admit terrorist murders – headline read by presenter.
3. Prime Minister facing crucial vote in the Commons.
4. Cash crisis for public libraries – taped reports from two different libraries around the country and interviews with library users.
5. Boy aged eleven sentenced to death in Pakistan for blasphemy – script and film from Pakistan.
6. Actor Stephen Fry disappeared after getting critical reviews of his performance in a new West End play – taped interview with passenger who saw him on a ferry, heading for France.
7. Man charged with murder of a boy aged seven and his teenage babysitter in a northern town – tape of the scene of the alleged murders and of the man's home.
8. American who arranged for the murder of a British girl jailed - still photograph of the guilty man was shown.
9. New body set up to investigate miscarriages of justice and refer cases back to the Appeal Court – library tape of people wrongly convicted and then released.
10. USA to evacuate the final United Nations peacekeeping forces and remaining aid workers from Somalia – videotape showing the evacuations beginning.

Getting the story: the reporter's view
How does TV find news?

- As in newspapers, the newsdesk will have a **diary** of events it expects to cover.
- There will also be **breaking stories,** such as crimes, disasters, events in Parliament, and recently issued statements from pressure groups, official organisations and individuals.
- Reporters will also be tipped off by **contacts.** For example, a disenchanted doctor may leak a report on the state of the National Health Service to a health correspondent he knows and trusts.
- Stories will also come in from **agencies,** check calls to **emergency services** and **other media.**

A group of BBC foreign correspondents was asked by the *Radio Times,* 'How do you find stories?' These are some of their answers:

- 'Generally, I report breaking news, so its obvious; if it's a war I head for the fighting.' (Jeremy Bowen, Middle East Correspondent.)
- 'With my eyes and ears.' (Fergal Keane, Asia Correspondent.)
- 'Local media, gossip, diaried events, or just going and finding the story once you're there.' (Bridget Kendall, Washington Correspondent.)
- 'By talking to people in countries where I think something unusual is happening.' (George Alagiah, Southern Africa Correspondent.)
- 'By scrutinising many daily papers, and by journalistic intuition.' (Brian Barron, New York Correspondent.)
- 'By talking to – or listening to – those who make the US Government tick.' (Gavin Esler, Chief North America Correspondent.)

Chasing the story
Before any news story can be broadcast, an enormous amount of information-gathering and checking has to be done. This is how one story might develop:

- A reporter with a regional TV station gets a **tip** that three patients have each had an eye removed after being infected during surgery at a local hospital. The tip comes from a union official at the hospital, early in the morning.

- The reporter **phones** the hospital immediately and asks to speak to the senior registrar. His request is denied and he is referred to the regional health authority press office.

- **Phone call no. 2**: the press office say they have no comment at present, but a statement will be issued at 4.30pm. This tells the reporter he is on to something, but he has nothing to go with on the lunchtime news.

- **10.30am**. He rings his contact and asks for more detail – anything that might help him find the patients.

- **11.10am**. Contact comes back with the name of one surgeon involved.

- **Reporter rings the surgeon** and asks him to comment. The surgeon at first says he has no comment, but inadvertently mentions the name of a patient.

- The reporter **goes back to the press office**, puts the name of the patient to them, and asks for a comment for the next bulletin. Meanwhile, he arranges for a camera crew to go to the hospital to tape some general scenes.

- **12.30pm**. Press office comes back with a terse statement, confirming that the named man had an eye removed as a result of infected equipment at the hospital. That's enough for a report to lead the lunchtime programme.

- **12.50pm**. Reporter joins camera crew at the hospital to make a videotaped report. It begins like this: 'A patient at Southwick Hospital has had an eye removed after a routine operation. Infected equipment is to blame. It's believed two other patients may also have lost an eye each . . .'

- **1.20pm**. His report goes out, and the programme cuts to him, live outside the hospital for a further update.

- By the **evening news**, he hopes to have found one or more of the patients and talked to them. There is still a lot of work ahead.

Putting a news programme together: BBC's *Six O'Clock News*

The large newsroom on the sixth floor of Television Centre in London is home to *Breakfast News*, the *One O'Clock News*, the *Six O'Clock News* and the *Nine O'Clock News*.

The newsroom is divided into two: newsgathering and output. Newsgathering has home and foreign desks, a news organiser and correspondents out on the road. It provides news for all the programmes above.

Staff correspondents are not the only sources of news. The foreign desk watches output from affiliated television stations around the world. The home desk can take a package from any regional BBC newsroom. It also monitors agencies, such as the Press Association.

The production of the *Six O'Clock News* is controlled from a large, central desk staffed by the programme editor, the newsreaders and the producers. That same desk is used by similar teams producing the '*One*' and the '*Nine*' as they are called. As one team finishes its daily programme and moves out, another moves in.

Television news works in '**newsdays**'. The newsday for the '*Six*' begins at **8.30am** when the programme team arrives at the office. They have already read the morning newspapers, listened to radio bulletins or watched *Breakfast News*.

- **At 9am**, the **first editorial conference** of the day takes place. It begins with a post-mortem on the previous day's programmes. Then it's on to today, and the home and foreign news editors go through their schedules.

- Stories are discussed and the cry goes out several times: 'But what **pictures** have we got?'

- At a few minutes to ten, a small group in one corner – all in headphones – are typing frantically onto the newsroom computer system. This is the **summaries desk,** who produce bulletins on the hour.

- As **12 noon passes**, the *One* team discuss their running order; the *Six* are still quite relaxed.

- **2.30pm**. The *One* are finished and the main desk is vacant for the *Six*. Everyone grabs a quick sandwich. The programme

Date: 5 May	Programme: Six O'Clock		28'10"
001 TITLES/HEADS	CRVI/TITLES	GC	1.00
003	ANNE + GENERIC INSET		0:00
007 KIDNAP	ANNE (INSET:MISSING GIRL)	TM	0:35
008 KIDNAP/SMITH	VT/ASTONS	TM	4:00
010 ELECTIONS	ANNE (INSET:COUNTY HALL)	AJ	0.35
011 ELECTIONS/SINGH	VT/ASTONS	AJ	3.25
013 ELECTIONS LIVE	ANNE INTS SINGH, COUNTY HALL	AJ	1.30
016 FARMERS	TIM (INSET:FARMING)	LM	0.25
017 SMITH 2-WAY	TIM (2-WAY EX BATH STUDIO)	LM	2.30
018 SACKING	ANNE (INSET:SACKED WOMAN)	LM	0.30
019 SACKING/LLOYD	VT/ASTONS	LM	2.30
022 SCHOOLS	TIM (INSET GV SCHOOL)	TM	0.35
023 SCHOOLS/SINGH	VT/ASTONS	TM	2.25
046 PROMOS **		GC	0.30
047 STORES	TIM (INSET:SHOPPERS)	AL	0:25
048 STORES/LLOYD	VT/ASTONS	AL	2.25
049 MOTHER	ANNE (INSET:COURTS)	LM	0.30
049 MOTHER/SMITH	VT/ASTONS	LM	2.20
051 CLOWNS	TIM (INSET:CHARITY)	AJ	0.30
052 CLOWNS/LIVE	BOND IN HIGH STREET	AJ	2.45
055 CLOSE/END HEADS	ANNE (INSET:GEN)	TM	0.45
056	TITLES		

This is the running order for an early evening news programme. On the left is the page number, for use by the director and others. The second column shows the story name (identifying its subject), and the name of the reporter. The next column indicates whether the presenter – Anne or Tim – is on screen or whether videotape and captions (VT/ASTONS) are in use. The final columns show the initials of the producer and the duration of the report. 2-way means that the presenter will interview the reporter live.

Fig. 11. TV news running order.

119

Story: shootings	Reporter: Khan
Presenter I/V	A family of four have been shot dead by an escaped prisoner who is still on the run tonight.
Still/prisoner photofit	Police have sealed ports and set up roadblocks in the hunt for Gerald Anderson. They've warned the public not to approach him.
Still/GV house	The Wilson family were found dead by neighbours this afternoon. They broke into the locked house after
Still/family	failing to see Maureen Wilson, her husband Graham or their children Fiona and Rodney.
Mix to VT/neighbours	

Television scripts are set out in two wide columns. On the left is technical information, such as what the viewer sees on screen – the presenter, videotape, live material. On the right are the words read by the presenter or reporter. I/V stands for in vision, VT for videotape, still is a still photograph.

Fig. 12. TV news script.

editor now has a tentative **running order** (see Figure 11). The producers are turning reports into packages. They are on the phone to correspondents or writing their intros to scripts (see Figure 12), arranging graphics, fixing up permission for filming, finding library footage and writing 'Astons' (on-screen captions, named after the machine that sets them). The producers are also adding technical details to scripts – when to show a graphic, when to cut from newsreader in the studio to videotape.

- Two **presenters** join the central desk and begin rewriting the intros in their own style. They discuss how to improve a story that went out on the *One.*

- **4pm. Second editorial conference**. The *Six* editor reads out her final running order. But it isn't really final . . .

- **4.45pm**. The senior duty editor writes promos – the teasing headlines halfway through the programme about what is coming up later.

- **5pm**. A **new story** breaks which will have to go high up the running order. Everything needs rearranging and something has to be dropped.

- **Another change**. There may be a package on a story that was only going to get 20 seconds...

- **And another problem**. There will only be track and rushes (unedited soundtrack and videotape) instead of the edited package expected on a different story. It will have to be edited here at the last minute.

- **5.30pm**. A live report from Bosnia replaces a scripted item... it's much longer.

- **5.40pm**. Everyone watches the ITN news.

- **5.55pm**. Into the **gallery**. The gallery is the production room from where the broadcast is controlled. A bank of screens show the presenters in the studio below, edited videotape ready for use, and outside broadcast units with their cameras trained on correspondents. In the gallery is the programme editor, technical staff, the producers and the director. The director, working from the running order, cues in newsreaders, videotape and live broadcasts.

- **6pm**. Titles, and the programme is off. But there is still time to change the running order and substitute new scripts. The *Six* team is still waiting for videotape to accompany a report due to go out at 6.21pm. It arrives... at 6.20. In the newsroom, a producer is still writing the script for the final item. That arrives too, and the standby item is struck off the list.

- The *Six* team's newsday ends. But for the *Nine* the frenetic part is just beginning.

More about current affairs

If news bulletins are snapshots of what has happened in a particular day, current affairs programmes are the stories behind the stories, the analysis and investigation of topical items. Some current affairs programmes include:

- *Correspondent*, BBC2. This is made up of dispatches from BBC correspondents around the world.
- *A Week In Politics*, Channel 4. Political analysis.
- *Breakfast With Frost*, BBC1. Interviews with prominent politicians.
- *Around Westminster*, BBC2. A review of the week's events in and around Parliament.
- *The Money Programme*, BBC2. Investigation and analysis of a topical financial or economic issue.
- *Westminster on Line*, BBC2. Phone-in show in which the public ask politicians questions.
- *Newsroom Southeast*, BBC1. Regional news/magazine programme for London and the south east reporting a variety of local stories and looking at relevant issues.
- *London Tonight*, Carlton. The equivalent ITV regional news/magazine programme for London.
- *Newsnight*, BBC2. Reports and analysis of the day's news.
- *World In Action*, ITV. A topical magazine programme concentrating on one issue.
- *Network First*, ITV. Documentary/investigation of one issue.
- *Dispatches*, Channel 4. Detailed, analytical report on current affairs.
- *Big City*, ITV. News and features about the world of entertainment.

Television current affairs covers a wide brief. Politics, economic issues, injustices – particularly where there is potent human interest – and investigations all feature. For example, the BBC current affairs programme *Panorama*, now over 40 years old, has broadcast programmes on:

- Robert Maxwell
- Terry Venables
- the sleeping drug Halcyon
- single mothers who reportedly had babies to increase their state benefits
- rape
- breast cancer

- drugs
- how schoolgirls are brighter than boys
- the Middle East peace process
- blood transfusions causing the passing on of Hepatitis C.

Panorama's editor, Steve Hewlett, told *The Guardian* in early 1995: 'We must cover the right topics in a user-friendly way by seeking an agenda in which people are interested.'

TELETEXT: FAST NEWS

'The potential in Teletext is tremendous and as more open up there will be more jobs for journalists.'

David Klein, Teletext editorial director,
(*UK Press Gazette*)

What is Teletext? Simply, text on a television screen. Teletext describes itself as 'a newspaper of the airwaves.'

Both BBC and ITV have Teletext systems. Pages of data – news, weather, travel information, sport, TV programme listings and many other kinds of material – are transmitted free. All the viewer needs is a television set capable of receiving teletext. Pages are selected using a remote control keypad.

How does Teletext reach the viewer?

News flows into the Ceefax newsroom at the BBC from the corporation's massive newsgathering machine. There, Teletext reports are written by sub-editors working to a chief sub and ultimately to an editor.

The Teletext newsroom at ITV is similar, except that news flows in from ITN and agencies such as the Press Association, Reuters and AP (Associated Press).

Teletext news reports are short and to the point, because only so much text will fit onto a television screen. However, some stories run to several pages.

Once the report is written it can be transmitted immediately, making Teletext the fastest form of news dissemination after radio.

As Britain's television channels proliferate, so too will Teletext services.

THE FUTURE: VIDEOJOURNALISTS.

'I've been a print journalist and I've worked in radio and as far
as I'm concerned, it's the future.'

Patrick O'Hagan, videojournalist.

(*ES Magazine, Evening Standard*)

A new kind of television reporter appeared on Britain's streets in
1994. They are videojournalists, who do everything reporters working
for traditional TV stations do, but more. 'VJs', as they quickly
became known, also film and edit their own material. A VJ will be
concerned not only with getting the story, but also with framing shots,
avoiding bland backgrounds, focusing, getting the colour right and
compensating for bad light. When they get back to the studio they
must edit their own tape as well as writing their scripts.

VJs are so far employed mainly by small cable companies. As
these companies set up operations in large cities throughout Britain,
there will be a growing demand for VJs.

One such station, Channel One, broadcasts in London. It began
with 30 staff VJs, plus freelance contributors. Its chairman, Sir
David English, promised it would be 'very immediate and
interactive'. The channel transmits rolling news bulletins, 24
hours a day. News is alternated with items on health, schools,
transport, crime or entertainment.

Reactions to this development

The first reaction to the new VJs was positive. Adam Sweeting said
in *The Guardian*: 'They immediately proved that the one-person-
with-camera approach can work, though some reporters proved
bolder than others at combining a camera in the face with an
accompanying blunt question. It was satisfying to see a harassed
local councillor being quizzed on why he had looked uncomfortable
in court, for example, even if he didn't answer.'

Mark Honingsbaum, writing in *ES magazine*, said: 'The station's
videojournalists ... have already begun to challenge one of television's most hallowed conventions: the idea that you need one man
to hold a tripod and another to ask the questions.'

It is predicted that the arrival of videojournalism could lead to
far-reaching changes in the way television news in general is
gathered and produced. So far, such dramatic changes have not
happened, but there will be plenty of jobs for those prepared to
travel with camcorder. Plans have already been laid for cable news

channels in Manchester, Sheffield, Newcastle, Birmingham, Leeds, Bristol and Liverpool.

CASE STUDIES

Editor, network current affairs programme

Mike is 37. Unusually, he has never trained as a journalist yet has a powerful and responsible job.

Mike was originally a lecturer in communication studies at a university in the south west. Trying to supplement his salary, he offered ideas to the editor of a magazine programme made by the regional television station in his area. One of his ideas made it into a programme and, as a consequence, he was taken on as a temporary researcher for six weeks during the summer vacation. He decided never to go back to lecturing and, when his temporary contract ended, he got a job with an ITV current affairs programme.

He quickly made up for his lack of formal training by generating innovative and hard-hitting ideas for programmes and mastering technical skills. For the next decade he moved from job to job in television current affairs. His reputation as an editor grew with each move. He masterminded an award-winning investigation into the scandal of a collapsed bank, which took with it millions of pounds of investments. He also edited a highly regarded programme on price-fixing by supermarkets which had brought higher costs to consumers. And he led an investigation into tax avoidance by senior civil servants.

He was offered his current post because the programme, with a long history of investigative journalism behind it, was thought to be slipping. Mike's brief is both to restore its reputation and increase its audience ratings. 'Television is the most powerful form of communication on earth,' he says. 'I want to see journalists using it wisely and responsibly.'

Newsreader, satellite channel

Mohit, 32, began like many television journalists – on local newspapers. She joined a weekly paper straight from school but quickly decided she wanted to move into broadcasting. Once she had qualified she applied for a job as a researcher, simply as a way in to television. She was working for a daytime, studio-based discussion programme, researching and writing briefings for the presenter on issues that would be put before the studio audience.

After two years, Mohit discovered that the station she was

working for had a vacancy in the newsroom. She took a written test, was given an interview and made a demonstration videotape – and got the job. At first she did general news reporting, going out of the studio with a camera crew to follow up local stories.

When she had been in the job for around two years, Mohit was given a chance to stand in as a newsreader at weekends. She had a natural aptitude for appearing on screen – a pleasant voice and appearance and a relaxed, professional attitude. She was popular with viewers and soon switched to newsreading full-time.

As well as appearing on screen, she writes her own headlines, intros and scripts. She reads a large number of newspapers and magazines so that she is informed about the stories of the day, and prepared for any live interviews she may have to do, often with little warning. She also sits in on editorial conferences, joining the discussion about the importance of the various stories on the schedule and suggesting ways of covering them.

'There's nothing like the buzz of live television. I could never go back to newspapers,' she says.

7

Other Choices

'The idea of being a freelance journalist, working on commission for several different people, is one that many find attractive. But nearly all freelance reporters, writers and sub-editors were staff journalists first. That is because, to be a freelance, you need to have learned the necessary skills, and you need to have built up contacts in journalism to whom you can sell your work.'

Careers in Journalism, National Union of Journalists

'It was probably about 6.00pm or 6.30pm last Thursday that Reuters broke the news that the world's most sought-after trader, Nick Leeson, had been detained in Frankfurt, and shortly after that London News Radio ran with the story before the BBC, thus hitting its mission statement – First, Live, London – fair and square. This was the big story of the day, and it played perfectly into the hands of LNR.'

Dominic Mills, *Campaign* (writing in March 1995)

NEWS AGENCIES

News agencies supply other media, usually a wide cross-section of print and broadcast organisations. They range in size from international agencies such as Reuters to small, two-men-bands in provincial towns and cities. Most cover a broad range of news and features, but some specialise in one area, such as court reporting or sport.

Agencies employ journalists much as other media do. They have editors, reporters, specialist writers, subs and photographers. And these journalists work in much the same way, finding stories, researching them, interviewing people, writing up their copy, and editing it. There is one important difference. Their stories must be sold on to other media.

How do agencies sell their work?

National and international agencies provide a news service to subscribers. A rolling file of news is transmitted to the customer who may use all or any of it. All major news events are covered by the agencies' own staff. News flows straight into the subscribers' own computer system.

With smaller agencies, individual stories are sold at a pre-negotiated price to one buyer.

In Britain, agencies are either of these two types: the large 'wire services' and smaller, local agencies.

National and international agencies: the wire services

These include PA (Press Association), Reuters, AP (Associated Press) and UPI (United Press International).

They are known as the 'wire services'. They transmit news stories throughout the day and night to subscribers such as national newspapers, the BBC and large regional newspapers.

The term 'wire services' dates from their transmission method before the computer era, when everything was telegraphed on paper from their offices to newspapers and broadcast media. Now, copy is fed directly into the computer system of the receiving organisation. It can then be accessed by all the organisation's journalists.

Britain's major national news agency, the Press Association, supplies news to a large number of national and provincial newspapers, television and radio stations. Reuters supplies newspapers, radio and television stations around the world.

First with the news

The wire services aim to provide comprehensive and accurate coverage, and to do it fast. They are often first with a major story. Dominic Mills, writing in *Campaign*, said that 'Reuters, of course, made its name by the speed and accuracy of its news coverage – when I worked there you were measured for speed against the competition in seconds.'

They use a code to indicate the importance of a breaking story:

- **Rush** – a major item such as the death of a world leader.
- **Flash** – an item of great importance.
- **Snap** – first news of an important event.

These will be transmitted as one-sentence reports at first, simply to alert subscribers to what has happened. Full versions of the story will then follow.

Other agencies

There are many other news agencies in Britain, much smaller and locally based. They may report on whatever is happening on their 'patch' or they may specialise. For example, one agency covers only cases being heard at the Central Criminal Court in London, supplying newspapers, radio and television. Another example would be the INS Agency with offices in Reading and Southampton, which reports on events in its area. It then sells its work to local and national newspapers, television and radio, and magazines. It also supplies photographs.

Such agencies exist in most large provincial towns and cities, each employing several journalists.

The BBC television series *Harry* portrayed life in a provincial news agency. Employing three writers and one photographer, the fictional agency, News Associates, concentrated on finding, writing and picturing stories it could sell to the tabloids. But life in a small news agency is not always as exciting as Harry's.

Photographs too

Most agencies provide photographs to accompany stories. Reuters, PA, AP and UPI have photographers around the world. Local agencies usually have at least one photographer, or employ photojournalists.

Some agencies offer extra services, such as information from a cuttings library, graphics and listings. Listings can be any kind of tabulated or listed information, from race cards to television programmes.

How do agency journalists work?

They do similar jobs to journalists on newspapers or in broadcasting, but the stories they cover depend entirely on the size and location of the agency. Journalists working for Reuters report news from around the world. Those working for the Press Association could cover a story anywhere in Britain or abroad. Journalists with an agency based in, for example, Leeds will cover local stories with a national angle.

How do agencies get the news out?

- *The international agencies* have bureaux around the world. For output in Britain, reporters and correspondents file their copy to the London bureau either by telephone or by computer. It will then be assessed on its news value, edited, given a headline and transmitted to subscribers.

• *The national news agency*, the PA, receives reports from its correspondents around Britain at its London office. Similarly it will edit them and transmit them to subscribers.

• *Local news agencies* will try to sell each story on its merits. Once the reporter has finished the article – or even before it is completed – the editor or news editor telephones news editors or features editors on newspapers and in radio and television to see if they are interested in the story. They may sell it exclusively to one organisation or offer it 'all round'. The copy will then be sent by computer or dictated by telephone.

Who buys agency news?

The answer is, almost every media organisation.

• *National* newspaper and national broadcast media tend to subscribe to agencies which major in foreign coverage, such as Reuters. They also take the PA output and buy stories they are interested in as they are offered by local agencies.

• *Local* newspapers and broadcast media often take the PA service and buy stories or tips from local agencies.

• *Financial and business news* has a special market. Companies and City institutions may take financial news provided by one of the wire services. There are also agencies specialising in this type of information, such as Extel Financial.

Example: one day at the Press Association

The PA transmits a full news service to its subscribers. It covers pre-planned events and breaking stories. It also transmits a sports service, law reports and features. Subscribers choose which services they want and pay accordingly.

PA employs reporters, specialist writers, sub-editors, section editors, photographers and lawyers. Its staff is structured in a similar way to that of a large, daily newspaper.

The excerpts from the schedules below show some of the stories the PA covered on a typical day in 1995. (*Note*: A 'nightlead' is a major story.)

PA
NIGHT SCHEDULE FOR WEDNESDAY JANUARY 11 1995

POLITICS Labour: Labour leader Tony Blair tore into his party's rebel Euro-MPs, accusing them of 'gross discourtesy' which wrecked his first European outing and 'blunted' his New Year message to the nation. Profile in file. Nightlead.

TRANSPORT Rail: A storm of protest has greeted proposals that could see the number of rail stations providing customers with through tickets cut to fewer than 300. Nightlead.

POLITICS Calves: Demonstrators picketed Swansea airport as it geared up for livestock exports while news emerged of another port, Brightlingsea, Essex, seeking to join the controversial trade. With section on police officers at Shoreham also unhappy with the trade in veal. Nightlead.

ROYAL Camilla: Royal biographer Jonathan Dimbleby said he did not expect the Prince and Princess of Wales to announce divorce plans in the foreseeable future.

LEGAL Aid: Radical proposals to change the 'inadequate' Legal Aid system were unveiled by the Lord Chancellor. With reaction. Nightlead.

CITY Saatchi: Maurice Saatchi announced he is to set up a new advertising agency as turmoil continued at Saatchi & Saatchi with more resignations just hours after attempts were launched to try to restore confidence in the group. Nightlead.

PRISON Escape: Prison governors held a meeting with Prison Service boss Derek Lewis this afternoon (1630) to demand an explanation for the treatment of the sacked Parkhurst governor and the prison's staff. Nightlead.

ECONOMY Factory: Factory output fell sharply in November, official figures showed. Nightlead.

INDUSTRY Jobs: Leading snack food producer United Biscuits is to close one of its factories with the loss of up to 980 jobs. Also:

INDUSTRY Cook: Travel Group Thomas Cook to axe 160 jobs in Poole with the closure of travellers cheque subsidiary but create 250 new jobs in Peterborough, company announced tonight. Nightlead.

TRIBUNAL Diggle: Angus Diggle, the lawyer jailed for trying to rape a fellow solicitor, was suspended from practice for a year by the solicitors' Disciplinary Tribunal today. Nightlead.

COURTS Christie's: Christie's, the fine art auctioneers, were ordered by a judge to repay £557,500 to the buyer of a painting which turned out to be a fake. In file.

FOREIGN
ZIMBABWE Doctor: Demonstrators called for long prison term as

Zimbabwe judge deferred sentencing in racially charged case of a Scottish doctor found guilty of killing two black patients with morphine. (1306)

PHILIPPINES Pope: Police arrested two people suspected of plot against Pope and warned of bomb threat against US airlines over the Pacific during John Paul's Asian visit this week. (0723)

RUSSIA Chechnya: Russia's Parliament met in special session to discuss Chechnya, quickly showed it was unwilling to halt military action. (0843)

US Milk: Supermodels Christie Brinkley, Iman and Naomi Campbell will be wearing white moustaches in a new ad campaign – for milk. (1420, with pic)

RWANDA Attack: Soldiers loyal to Rwanda's ousted government raided a remote fishing village in first big attack since they fled into exile. (1422)

SPORT

The Plymouth–Peter Shilton saga reached a head today, with the former England goalkeeper quitting as the second division club's manager and declaring he would not be attending the club's disciplinary hearing tomorrow.

The future of FAW chief executive Alun Evans is under the spotlight at the association's special meeting in Caersws.

Tonight is Coca Cola cup quarter-final night with Bolton–Norwich, Crystal Palace–Man City, Liverpool–Arsenal and Swindon–Millwall.

NEWSFEATURES

WAR: The horrific story of Auschwitz was graphically told in the film *Schindler's List*. Now the movie has been released for video rental to mark the 50th anniversary of the concentration camp. Cathy Gordon meets a survivor of Auschwitz, Trude Mosonyi-Levi, who tells of the horrors of the camp and how it has affected all those who survived.

PHOTO SCHEDULE

Times as diary, not running times.
Items expected:
Soccer:
Coca Cola cup quarter-finals:
1930 Bolton Wanderers v Norwich City
1945 Crystal Palace v Manchester City
1945 Liverpool v Arsenal

Pictures in today's file include:
- Naomi Campbell and Lauren Bacall appear with a milk moustache in a new $52 million campaign (two pix, both vertical).

- Injured England fast bowler Darren Gough rests in his hotel after breaking a bone in his left foot (vert).
- A woman just five feet tall has surprised medical staff by giving birth to a baby two feet tall.
- P&O's £200 million superliner Oriana nearing completion at a German shipyard (vert).
- Spring lingerie collection from Gossard (both formats).
- Filer of Peter Shilton who has resigned as manager of Plymouth FC.
- Two Chechen fighters spring from the Presidential Palace through the rubble created by incessant Russian bombing in Grozny (horiz).
- Storms in California (both formats).
- Police issued E-Fit of a man who kidnapped a teenage girl from Ness, South Wirral (vert).

FREELANCING

What is a freelance?
'He travels the fastest who travels alone.'

Rudyard Kipling, *The Winners*

There are thousands of freelance journalists working in Britain. In 1994, the NUJ alone had 6,000 freelance members. Technically, any journalist who is not on the staff of a media organisation is a freelance. Journalists working alone and selling articles to the media are freelances.

Freelances are not paid a salary and do not receive benefits payable to permanent staff, such as sickness pay, private health insurance, pension rights or company cars. They are paid a set fee simply for the work they supply.

However, the situation is more complicated than that. Some staff journalists also do freelance work for other media. For example, a BBC contract presenter may also write magazine articles; a national newspaper specialist writer may also present a 'what the papers say' television programme. Television presenters are increasingly writing newspaper columns as well; they include Anne Robinson in the *Daily Express* and Vanessa Feltz in the *Daily Mirror*.

Some freelances also have contracts to work for a certain organisation for a specific period. They can also be contracted to write a certain number of articles per year. Others are paid a 'retainer' to write so many articles in a given period and also to be on standby in case they are needed.

The crucial difference between staff and freelance journalists is that a staff job pays a regular salary, whereas freelances are paid only for what they supply.

Many locally based agencies are staffed by only one or two journalists working on a freelance basis.

How do freelances work?

Freelancing involves selling stories or features to any of the media. This can be done in one of two ways. Either the journalist can get a story, write it up and offer the finished version to publications and broadcast media. This is called working **on spec**. Or he or she can offer them a piece on the basis of an idea. The freelance negotiates a price for a certain number of words before proceeding with the article. This is called working **on commission**.

In either case, freelance journalists rely heavily on contacts they have built up within media organisations. It is extremely difficult for an unknown freelance to sell material, but, of course, everyone has to start somewhere.

Most freelances have previously held a staff post in which they would have learned the basics of journalism and built up something of a reputation. When they go it alone, they can then introduce themselves as having previously worked for such-and-such a publication. This lets their potential buyer know that they have been trained and are experienced journalists.

However, in theory anyone can set up as a freelance. There is no legal requirement to be fulfilled before beginning work. But any aspiring freelance would be well advised to get a proper grounding in the laws of libel and contempt, guidelines on privacy, and basic journalistic skills such as news reporting and feature writing before taking such a step.

How do freelances find stories?

Professional journalists work in much the same way, whatever their field. The chapters on newspapers, radio and television give much information about newsgathering. To recap briefly, they find stories from:

- **Public hearings** such as courts, councils and industrial tribunals.

- Talking to **contacts** (people the journalist knows in the community).

- **Other media**: for example, a journalist might write for a newspaper or magazine about a forthcoming television programme shot in his or her local area. Or a freelance might spot a story in a local paper which can be developed for the national press.

- **News events** in the area. These can be covered as they happen. The journalist would find out about them from regular check calls to the emergency services and from tips.

- Using **personal** expertise or experience as the basis for articles. For example, a journalist who also does do-it-yourself might contribute to a 'homes and gardens' style magazine. A journalist who is a working mother might write about her experiences for a parenting magazine.

The right story for the right market

There are markets in all the media for the work of freelance journalists. Selling work is easier if that journalist has contacts within newspapers, magazines, radio or television, but it is possible simply to offer an unsolicited piece and find a buyer.

Freelances must study possible markets and target their work towards them. They need to know what subjects are covered by which publication so that they do not make the mistake of offering the wrong type of material. For example, there is no point offering a travel article to a women's magazine which does not cover travel. And it would be a waste of time offering a piece about a collector of classic cars to a motorbike magazine.

A major part of a freelance's work is studying as wide a range of newspapers and magazines as he or she can get hold of. Reading other publications often sparks off ideas for articles, and equips the freelance to know what to offer where. They must also study as many radio and television current affairs programmes as they can and become familiar with which independent production companies make programmes on which subjects. All this means work can be specifically targeted, which gives it a better chance of acceptance.

There are also reference books such as *The Writer's Handbook* which list publications and broadcast organisations with their areas of interest and advice on how to approach them. Some of these are listed in the Further Information section at the end of this book.

Getting the style right

Freelances will also need to be familiar with the 'style' of the publication they are proposing to submit work to. By style, journalists mean the kind of writing that is common to a publication. For example, broadsheet newspapers tend to prefer longer articles written in longer sentences and do not allow slang to be used. Tabloid newspapers, however, go for shorter pieces, written in short, sharp sentences and peppered with direct quotes.

It is essential for an aspiring freelance to study the style of any media he or she wants to work for.

How do you sell a story?

Freelances offer stories by phone, fax or letter. If it is an on-the-day news story, the freelance telephones the newsdesk of newspapers, radio stations or television newsrooms that he thinks might be interested. He gives a brief outline of the story and the desk journalist will agree to buy it or say no. If it is wanted, the number of words and a fee will be agreed.

If it is a feature or a series of features, the journalist can fax or write to features editors on magazines or producers/editors in broadcast organisations. Again, a fee and the amount of work the freelance is expected to do will be agreed.

What about getting paid?

The National Union of Journalists lays down minimum rates of pay for its members. But freelances are free to try to negotiate more. After submitting work, they will send an invoice for the agreed amount. Here are some examples from the NUJ minimum rates:

- News reports for BBC local radio – £17.84 for the first two minutes, and £6.42 for each extra minute.
- News reports for BBC television – £42.98 for two minutes, and £10.66 for each extra minute.
- BBC Radio features and documentaries – £151 for seven minutes, then £21.70 per extra minute.
- Magazines including *GQ*, *Just Seventeen*, *Marie Claire* and *Vanity Fair* – £220 per thousand words for features.
- National daily newspapers – £155 per thousand words for reviews; £200 per thousand words for features.
- Public relations – working in press office, £100 per day.
- Provincial newspapers – sports reports, £17 for 100 words.

Getting started

To freelance, you must have:

- A basic knowledge of reporting and feature writing.
- Familiarity with the laws of libel and contempt and guidelines on privacy.
- Ideas for stories or features.

On a practical front, the minimum you will need are:

- Somewhere to work. Many freelances start by working from home.
- A telephone.
- Typewriter or, better still, personal computer.
- Reference books, including a dictionary, local guides and directories.

Also extremely useful are:

- Fax machine.
- Modem to allow you to transmit copy direct from your computer to the receiving organisation.
- Tape recorder.

Who would make a good freelance?

If you aim to become a freelance you will need all the personal qualities demanded of staff journalists, and more.

- You will need to be able to motivate yourself.
- You will need bags of self-confidence.
- You will be good at working alone, at managing your time, at organising your own office and doing your own accounts.
- Most importantly, you will have to be superb at making contacts who will give you stories, for without exclusive stories you are unlikely to earn a good living.

The freelance does many jobs in one day – investigative reporter, feature writer, editor, researcher and salesman or saleswoman. But there is one considerable **advantage**, and that is that you are answerable only to yourself.

Other ways of finding work

A freelance makes most of his or her income from originating ideas and turning them into saleable stories, features or scripts.

However, work for freelances is sometimes advertised. Perhaps a newspaper needs an extra sub-editor while a member of staff is away, or perhaps there is a special project to be carried out, a supplement to be written and subbed or a book to be put together. You can find this type of work advertised along with staff jobs in *The Guardian*'s media pages and in *UK Press Gazette*. Here are some examples:

Freelance/contributing editor needed: future possibility of full-time position.
A quarterly publication launched last month needs a regular editor at the helm. It is not a full-time position but there are good opportunities for the right person. You will need good journalistic experience and a knowledge of all aspects of publishing. Send brief CV.

Freelance researchers
Living in London, required to work on international reference book. Must be fluent in at least one other EU language. Apply in own handwriting.

Freelance editors and art editors
International publisher is looking for freelance editors and art editors to work on new product development. You must be creative, well-organised, flexible, numerate and resourceful; above all you will enjoy researching and working with concepts to create products that combine a visual approach of the highest quality with editorial depth and substance.

Editors must be able to write, sub-edit, manage schedules and budgets and will be proficient in QuarkXpress. Art editors will require a thorough knowledge of QuarkXpress, Illustrator and Photoshop.

Please send CV with a covering letter.
(*Note*: QuarkXpress is a software programme.)

WORKING ABROAD

'The women who work out in the free-fire zone of foreign reporting have heard it all: from the know-nothings who call them wanton, pushy, unfeminine, sexless, shrill, aggressive, abrasive, strident; from readers and viewers who worry about the 'girls' at the front, and from old-timers ... who allegedly said no woman could be a foreign correspondent because their voices are too high.'
'Our Women In Moscow', Reggie Nadelson, *You Magazine*

There are opportunities for British journalists to work abroad in many countries including Australia, the United States, Europe, Canada, South Africa and the Gulf States. You will not necessarily need to be fluent in a foreign language, but obviously it does help in a non-English speaking country. Working abroad can be done either as:

- A staff foreign correspondent for a British media organisation.
- A staff employee on a foreign publication.
- A freelance, selling to all media, British and foreign.

Before you consider working abroad, find out as much as you can about working practices and conditions in the country you have in mind. You must be fully informed about your eligibility to work there before you even think of boarding a plane.

It is wise to consult the Department of Social Security about preserving pension rights and entitlement to other benefits while you are away. You should also check up on your liability to UK income tax.

Get advice from the journalists' organisations including the National Union of Journalists and the Chartered Institute of Journalists.

Jobs abroad are available in the print media, radio, television and public relations. Many jobs will be for news correspondents but some will be for specialists, such as financial writers and broadcasters.

Some companies in certain countries, particularly the Middle East, may offer accommodation and fringe benefits, such as paid travel for home visits, tax-free salaries and education allowances. The period of employment offered may be fixed or open-ended; terms and conditions obviously vary widely.

Staff foreign correspondents

These are journalists employed by British media, such as the BBC, but posted to cities abroad for a fixed period. Their salary and conditions are agreed before the posting begins and they work solely for the organisation who sent them to a foreign location. For more information on foreign correspondents, see Chapters 3 and 6 on newspapers and television.

Working for foreign media

English-language newspapers exist in many parts of the world and do recruit British journalists. As an example, Jonathan Fenby, editor of *The Observer* until early 1995, was appointed editor of the *South China Morning Post* based in Hong Kong. The former editor of *Today*, Martin Dunn, moved across the Atlantic and edited the *New York Daily News*. The British journalist Tina Brown edits *New Yorker* magazine.

America attracts a large number of British journalists, many of whom work in California and Florida, making a good living writing stories and features about Hollywood celebrities for the British media.

Freelancing abroad

This is the most difficult option – simply deciding on a location, setting up there and then trying to find your customers. It is not impossible, but it needs careful research and meticulous planning.

First, choice of location

The journalist may choose a city as a base because of a forthcoming event, for example, the Olympics – or because he or she speaks the appropriate language. When choosing where to go ask these questions:

1. What potential is there for finding good stories? Is it a large metropolitan area? Are there any major events coming up? Is there a British connection, such as a forces base, or a British community? Is it the seat of government or of any international organisations? Will what happens there be of interest in Britain?

2. How easy is it to meet British deadlines? For example, is there a large time difference, as with the Far East or the United States?

3. Will I be able to find and afford somewhere to live and work? For example, accommodation in Hong Kong is prohibitively expensive for a freelance journalist.

Then find your customers

Having made a choice of location, the next job is to try to find news organisations who may buy your output. Long before heading off abroad, it is a good idea to write to as many news editors/foreign editors as possible, explaining where you are intending to set up as a freelance and offering to supply them with copy. Try to set up meetings with them if possible; that way, they are far more likely to remember who you are, rather than simply filing your letter.

Try also to get some firm commissions before you go. Think up some ideas for pieces that you could do from your new base and offer them to features editors on newspapers, magazines and in radio and television. Then, at least you will have some work to start you off.

Building up contacts

Once you arrive, let your presence be known. Contact local organisations and establish yourself as a bona fide freelance. Also contact other British journalists in the area, and see if you can co-operate.

Speak to local publications and broadcast media, offering them your services or any specific articles you have in mind.

Make sure you have enough money to last you for several months before even attempting to freelance abroad; it will be some time before you get much income. And remember that freelancing abroad is not a venture for the faint-hearted. It is probably easier if undertaken with a partner, either another journalist or a photographer.

PUBLIC RELATIONS

'PR is not, as some people imagine, a suspect whitewashing activity, but is "the deliberate, planned and sustained effort to establish and maintain mutual understanding between an organisation and its public." '

Careers in the Media, Julia Allen (Kogan Page)

Public relations is a career in its own right. Why include it in a book about working in journalism? Simply because many journalists eventually move into public relations, where they can has make use of their inside knowledge about how the media operate. There is almost no crossover the other way – experience in public relations is unlikely to get you a job in journalism.

The two professions work closely together. Public relations practitioners give stories to journalists through press releases, tips and setting up interviews. Journalists use public relations people when they want a quote or a response from an organisation, when they want to interview a public figure or figurehead and when they want basic information.

Most major organisations have a public relations department. PR men or women are sometimes known as press officers. Those who employ press/PR officers include the Prime Minister, the Metropolitan Police, the royal family, the BBC, government information services, companies, charities and organisations of all kinds.

Public relations practitioners also work for large consultancies, who have a variety of clients. The job has close links to advertising and marketing.

How does a PR practitioner work?
The PR officer has two threads to his or her activity:

- To be **proactive**, disseminating information to the media.
- To be **reactive**, commenting on events.

The proactive role is to promote a positive image of the organisation or individual being represented. This is done through:

- Issuing press releases to newspapers and broadcast organisations.
- Being the public face of the organisation in the media; for example, answering questions at a public meeting.
- Organising exhibitions and presentations.
- Overseeing advertising campaigns.
- Organising media visits.
- Writing and/or editing a house magazine.

The reactive function means:
- Commenting on events within the organisation or on outside events which concern it in response to queries from the media.
- Advising personnel on dealing with the media.

The news conference
This is a key tool for a PR practitioner. Whenever he or she wants to announce an initiative or respond to an event, a news conference is a quick, effective way of doing so.

The PR officer organises the conference – arranging speakers, selecting visuals – and targets suitable journalists or photographers to invite.

For example, a company might hold a news conference to announce that it is to sponsor a major sporting series.

The press release
Press releases are another useful device. The PR practitioner uses them to make announcements – such as that a company has a new chairman or woman – and also to comment on relevant events (see Figure 13).

ANDY ROUTLEDGE – A NEW SINGLE

The new single by Andy Routledge, 'Black City', will be released on 18 July. His world tour begins on 30 July in London and takes him to New York, Los Angeles, Berlin, Paris, Barcelona and Tokyo – among others. Andy will be back in this country in November for a series of dates.

'Black City' was co-written by Jonathan Turner and produced by Li Lee Ho. It will feature on Andry's forthcoming album, *Winds Of Desire*, due for issue in September. For more information, review CD and interview requests, contact:

JACKIE LYNN or PETER DRUMMOND at PR Unlimited.

Fig. 13. A press release.

For example, the Law Society might issue a press release attacking proposed changes to the rules about who can claim legal aid. They might arrange a news conference too.

Who makes a good PR practitioner?
You will need to have the ability to write clearly and concisely, be a good communicator and a diplomat and be able to think quickly under media pressure.

Some examples of the **tasks** a PR practitioner might have to carry out include:

- *The charity PR*: organising a news conference to draw public attention to famine in a Third World country, with the aim of getting donations of money and goods.

  This would involve drawing up a list of journalists/ photographers to invite, selecting visuals such as photographs or videos to show at the conference and arranging for the director of the charity to speak and then answer journalists' questions. This might be followed up by the PR officer arranging for some journalists to visit the area.

- *The police PR*: responding to claims in a newspaper that police caused the death of a woman arrested for shoplifting.

  This might involve issuing a press release containing a statement from the chief constable or other senior officer, arranging a news conference at which senior officers could be questioned by journalists, fixing up a meeting between the family of the dead woman and senior police officers.

- *The company PR*: dealing with false rumours in the City that the company is about to be taken over. This might involve arranging for journalists to be given information which contradicts the rumours. A group of financial correspondents could be invited to have lunch with the company chairman and given an off-the-record briefing. They could also be given unpublished figures showing the healthy state of the company.

The ways into PR

Any school-leaver interested in a PR career does not need to qualify in journalism first because undergraduate and postgraduate qualifications in PR are available.

However, it is an opportunity for an experienced journalist wanting a change of direction. A large number of PR practitioners are former print or broadcast journalists. It is common for them to set up as freelance PRs, one of their functions being to produce house magazines for companies and organisations.

WORKING IN BOOKS

'Literature is the art of writing something that will be read twice; journalism what will be grasped at once.'

Cyril Connolly, journalist (1903–1974)

Books have not traditionally been regarded as part of the 'media', yet there are a number of journalists working in publishing. In a National Union of Journalists membership survey in 1994, 5.1 per cent of those responding worked in books; a further 1.4 per cent worked in a combination of magazines and books.

Journalists working in books are usually editors rather than writers (although many print and broadcast journalists eventually become authors too). Their duties could be any or all of the following:

- Reading and editing manuscripts.
- Checking proofs.
- Liaising with designers, illustrators, indexers and printers.
- Commissioning new work.

Getting started

Publishers recruit school- and college-leavers, either with good A-levels or with a degree. Languages are a bonus, because publishing is an international business.

Training by employers is almost always done on the job, but it is possible to take courses in various aspects of book publishing before applying for jobs.

The different jobs are:

Editorial assistants

The lowliest job, and the point of entry for many. They carry out a multitude of tasks such as research, proof-reading, writing captions and updating books for future editions.

Editors

Other journalists work as sub-editors and copy editors, checking manuscripts and preparing them for printing, much as a newspaper sub-editor does with a story for publication. They may rewrite sections of the book, or suggest to the author that he or she does it. They look at the manuscript in detail for mistakes in grammar, punctuation and spelling, and for poor writing. They can also choose the illustrations and write captions for them. And they may be involved in the design for the book jacket, and for the promotional copy about the author which appears inside the cover.

Commissioning editors
This is a job for someone with substantial experience of publishing. Their job is to find new authors and/or new work for successful publication. They will also negotiate with the publishing house's existing authors and/or their agents. Commissioning editors need a vast network of contacts in the publishing industry. They also need to be extremely widely read and well-informed about the book market. They are likely to visit major book fairs several times a year.
    Finding new books to publish is done by:

- Reading unsolicited manuscripts.
- Talking to agents, who may offer new work.
- Discussing new projects with existing authors.
- Identifying trends in publishing, and commissioning specific books.

The commissioning editor may also be involved in negotiating and drafting contracts, managing budgets for production of certain books, supervising freelance editors and designers and attending book launches and signings.

What qualities do you need?
- *Editors* must be widely read, have good general knowledge, be able to recognise good writing, and be well organised. They must also be able to deal with people at all levels – from authors to printers to book club buyers.

- *Commissioning editors* need a sixth sense akin to the newspaper journalist's instinct for news; they must be able to recognise trends in book buying which can be exploited and to assess whether a submitted manuscript is a winner or a loser. It is a difficult, if not impossible, task.

- *All editors* also need to be able to work under pressure. The book world is subject to deadlines just as is the rest of the media, but obviously because of the length and quality of the work a deadline may be months away. There is still mounting pressure, but it is not quite as relentless as in those jobs where deadlines are faced daily.

- *Copy editors* need an eye for detail, an excellent memory and high powers of concentration. Mistakes in books can have disastrous consequences; a serious error about someone featured in a book could give rise to a libel action and lead to the pulping of an entire print run.

- *Editorial assistants* simply need to be prepared to have a go at whatever they are asked to do, and to carry out the task methodically and competently.

Journalists as authors

Many journalists write books, either factual or fiction. Julie Burchill, formerly the *Sunday Times* film reviewer, is also a successful novelist. So is Celia Brayfield, who previously worked in newspapers. John Parker, a former senior journalist with the then Mirror Group Newspapers, writes royal biographies and other books. The presenter of BBC 2's *Newsnight*, Jeremy Paxman, has written books on subjects as diverse as the British establishment and fishing. Many political journalists write books on people in Parliament; foreign correspondents often write books describing their experiences, and sports journalists write biographies and anecdotal books allied to their chosen field.

How do journalists become authors?

- They have an idea for a work, approach a publisher and are contracted to produce it.

- *Or* a publishing house wants a certain book written and approaches a journalist with the specialist knowledge required.

Some typical job advertisements

Managing editor

This senior position requires outstanding management and organisational skills. The successful candidate must have at least two to three years' experience working on children's illustrated fiction and non-fiction and must have a real passion for children's books. The post involves managing a team of in-house and freelance editors, providing direction and motivation, and producing the highest quality books on schedule and on budget. Salary range £20,000 to £25,000.

Desk editor

We are a leading international publisher of academic and professional books and journals in the humanities and social sciences. We are looking for a desk editor to work on reference titles, including encyclopaedias and dictionaries. The job involves responsibility for managing the progress of new titles from typescript stage to finished copies; controlling schedules and budgets; liaising with authors; managing freelance copy editors and proofreaders; and managing and developing the use of new technology. Apply with CV and current salary.

CASE STUDIES

The journalist/author

Alistair had a distinguished career in newspapers lasting around 35 years. He began as a reporter on a national daily after leaving Oxford and rose through the ranks to become deputy editor. He was then appointed to edit a leading morning regional newspaper.

At the age of 48, the publishers decided they wanted a younger man, so he left. At that point he felt he would like to try a different career, so began writing books.

One of his many past jobs had been as a royal correspondent and Alistair had a good inside knowledge of the royal family. He had also kept all cuttings of the major stories he had written – a wealth of material. He decided to use that knowledge in a series of biographies of members of the royal family. The first was about the Queen Mother, and sold extremely well. He followed that with one on the Duke of Edinburgh, taking just over a year to complete each book. He is now planning a biography of the Queen, followed by the Prince of Wales, Prince Andrew and Prince Edward.

After his first book was issued, he became something of a 'royal expert', being asked by newspapers, television and radio to comment when royal stories broke. Because of his knowledge spanning a long period, he was able to offer insight and analysis into dramatic events, such as the breaking down of two royal marriages.

He now also has a contract with one national newspaper to write features on royal issues and events.

Reporting from abroad

Greg and Linda are both British, in their late twenties and have recently married. They are based in Los Angeles, where they have permits to work for publications around the world, excluding the United States. This protects the jobs of US journalists.

They met while both were reporters for a national tabloid newspaper, based in London. They quickly agreed that they would like to spend some time abroad and, as neither speaks a foreign language, opted for America.

They write stories and features for newspapers and magazines in Britain, Australia, South Africa, Canada and other English-speaking countries. Much of their work is based around California's showbusiness culture. They follow up stories from American magazines and newspapers; have their own contacts in the film industry who tip them off about stories; and they travel to other parts of the United States to report on general news of interest outside the USA.

On one assignment, they travelled to the island of Antigua where a British MP was enjoying a private holiday with a controversial companion, a financial adviser facing criticism for loss of clients' money. The object was to gain an interview with one or both parties; eventually Greg and Linda managed to get a table in a restaurant next to the holiday-makers, and were able to strike up a conversation with them. They persuaded the pair to grant them a formal interview the next day and, as a result, got their side of the story which was sold to every national newspaper in Britain.

American culture provides Linda with enough material to write a monthly column for a British magazine concentrating on entertainment and leisure. In it, she reports on the view from America, including gossip, information about new films, television series and books which will shortly arrive in the UK. Greg and Linda plan to spend a maximum of five years in the USA, before returning home to freelance. They do not now want to take staff jobs anywhere – they say they enjoy the freedom of working for themselves too much.

Freelance soccer reporter
Frank came into journalism late after a career in economic forecasting. His passionate interest in soccer led him to begin covering minor football matches for his local paper.

He then started selling his reports to magazines and to larger regional papers. Initially, it was a spare-time occupation but after two years he found the demand for his work growing. He left his full-time job and set up as a freelance, joining the National Union of Journalists and a sportswriters' association. He now covers matches in his local area for a wide variety of print, radio and local television; he also writes on issues surrounding football.

He has won an award for one piece of reporting. That was when a national Sunday newspaper asked him to help carry out an investigation into secret payments to club managers to ease the transfer of players. He worked on the story for several months with two staff journalists. It culminated in an exposé of secret payments throughout the game.

Frank had another good exclusive which appeared in every national newspaper and on most radio and television bulletins when the manager of a local club resigned suddenly, blaming fans' violence for driving him out of the game.

Frank is now working on two books. One features his own reminiscences about soccer matches he finds particularly memorable. The second is the history of a Premier League soccer club, based on interviews with past and present players and officials.

Frank works from his home, usually driving less than 100 miles in a round trip to cover matches. Sometimes he travels to away games. He has good contacts in all his local soccer clubs, but it is really his extensive knowledge of and enthusiasm for the game that keeps him in work.

Rock and pop writer

When she left school Michaela, 28, got a job in the music industry, as personal assistant to a public relations executive for a record company. After several years, knowing the business well, she decided she wanted to write about it, so applied for a job on a music magazine.

She began reporting on all aspects of the music industry such as new recording contracts, reviewing concerts and interviewing celebrities. A year later, however, the magazine closed because of falling circulation.

Michaela applied for jobs on other magazines and wrote to several editors, but she was unable to find a new staff post. Working with a friend and colleague from the magazine which closed, she set up as a freelance. The pair now share a rented office just out of central London and are successful at selling stories and features, mainly to the music press but occasionally to national newspapers.

Michaela has just started reviewing some rock and pop concerts for the quality broadsheets, standing in when their regular reviewers are unavailable. Her colleague, Anne, has decided to specialise in celebrity interviews, and spends much time trying to persuade public relations men and women to allow her an hour (or even a half hour) with a visiting star. She has had three or four exclusive interviews which she was able to sell to a Sunday paper colour magazine, a high-circulation, glossy gossip magazine, a daily newspaper and a London arts magazine.

Both partners in the agency work six or seven days a week. When they are not actually chasing a story or an interview, they are scouring the music press printed at home and abroad for ideas or taking contacts for lunch or a drink. Their day begins at around 10am and finishes in the early hours after they have been to a concert or a nightclub.

Michaela says: 'The rock business is a constant source of great stories and outrageous characters – we'll never run out of stuff to write about.'

8

Issues for Journalists

'You cannot hope to bribe or twist
Thank God, the British journalist.
But, seeing what the man will do
Unbribed, there's no occasion to.'
Humbert Wolfe, *The Uncelestial City*

'On the whole, we get the news we deserve. We like conflict,
and we like gossip about public figures. Norman Lamont's
black eye and visits to an off-licence were more interesting to
us than his views on Europe.'
Roger Bolton, *New Statesman*

A CHANGING PROFESSION

Journalism is constantly changing, much as society develops. Issues
concerning journalists are debated in public and, as a result,
working practices and standards change. Such changes can have an
effect on the day-to-day job of the journalist. This chapter looks at
some of the issues now on the journalists' agenda.

WHAT MAKES NEWS?

The question, what makes news? confronts every journalist every
day. That is not new and journalists have always had to decide what
is newsworthy. In the 1990s a debate has been taking place about
whether the press and broadcast organisations should report more
'good' as well as 'bad' news.

What is news?

The traditional definition of news was summed up in the 1960s as:

'a big event, which was easily understood, clearly relevant to
the audience, and not too out of the ordinary (unless it was
totally unexpected), occurring in one of the major nations,
preferably involving somebody already well known, who could

152

be photographed, and happening in time to make the media's deadlines. If it were a negative story, so much the better, largely because that made any event stand out and appear unambiguous.'

Michael Bromley, *Teach Yourself Journalism*, 1994

The stories which traditionally made front pages fitted this description; man-made and natural disasters, scandals involving public figures and crime.

Most journalists now agree that is too narrow a definition. One editor, Arthur McEwan, of the *San Francisco Examiner*, summed up the viewpoint when he said 'news is whatever a good editor chooses to print.'

News no longer has to be an event; it can be the result of an investigation, a human interest story, a prophetic statement, a campaign and even a picture.

How do journalists decide what makes news?

First, they use their instinct. Second, they use market research.

Newspapers frequently commission surveys and use groups of readers to tell them what is right and wrong with the paper. The results help them decide what to print.

However, many journalists say instinct is more important than statistics. They believe they can decide what is news based on studying popular culture in the form of television and radio, feedback from readers, families, friends and people met in the course of doing their job, and from their own experience.

News has become whatever is likely to interest a reader or a viewer.

Hard and soft news

In the past two decades 'soft' news has increasingly taken space from 'hard' news in the tabloid press.

What is the difference? **Hard news** is the 'big event' referred to earlier, a sudden, important, possibly shocking event which will have repercussions.

Soft news focuses on television and entertainment, and human interest; stories about showbusiness personalities, and about ordinary people involved in extraordinary situations.

Good or bad news?

Do newspapers and broadcast media concentrate too much on 'bad' or negative news? They do, according to the television journalist Martyn Lewis who said journalists should report more 'good' news. Journalists are divided about whether Mr Lewis has a point or not.

Some editors of provincial newspapers would agree. Many are changing their content to fight declining circulations. One of the changes is in reporting more 'good' news.

In the 1980s many provincial newspapers followed the look and style of the highly successful *Sun*. They adopted a 'shock, horror' approach to reporting and design. In the 1990s, they started finding 'good' news to report. In their case, 'good' news is community news and information.

The new thinking was summed up by Keith Sutton, editor of the *Evening News and Star*, based in Carlisle, and of the *Cumberland News*.

'We are close to our readers. We report their births, marriages and deaths, planning applications, motoring offences, whist drives, football matches. We bump into them in shops and pubs. In Carlisle, we also keep a "readers' comments" book on our newsdesk; we send out accuracy surveys every week to our contacts mentioned in articles asking them how accurately they have been reported.'

New Statesman

So far, national newspapers, radio and television still report mostly traditional 'hard' news. But the future is difficult to predict.

MULTI-SKILLING

'I have high hopes of the new style newsroom, in which we no longer send our least experienced people out to gather the news at first hand and encourage the office-bound to "correct" their copy. The abolition of journalists who, in H. L. Mencken's words, do not feel the wind of the world in their faces should bring papers closer to their readers.'

Nicholas Herbert, *UK Press Gazette*

In the 1980s newspapers went through a revolution. Newsrooms and the production process were computerised, vastly changing journalists' working methods and removing the power of the print unions.

In the 1990s, journalists faced more changes in the way they work. The trend was towards a single journalist having several sets of skills.

Traditionally, the role of the journalist was either as a **news-gatherer** – reporters, specialist and feature writers – or as a **news processor** – section editors, sub-editors, production staff. The trend now is journalists to combine different skills or switch roles.

- **In broadcasting**, it is increasingly common for journalists to work for both radio and television; some are beginning to film their own reports.

- **In newspapers**, change is gathering pace. Nicholas Herbert, the retiring deputy chief executive of Westminster Press, told the *UK Press Gazette*: 'Across the screen on which I show people Westminster Press's experimental electronic newspaper move the words "Change is now the status quo." '

- **In some provincial newspapers** the demarcation between reporter and sub-editor has vanished. Several regionals have adopted what is known as the 'orbital newsroom', described earlier (see Chapter 3).

Journalists are divided on the benefits of these changes and, so far, national newspapers are still mostly run along traditional lines. With bi-media broadcasting, too, some journalists have reservations. Unions with members working for the BBC have fought against them.

It is nevertheless clear that more changes – if not quite what employers want – are going to occur in journalists' lives.

WHO WATCHES THE JOURNALISTS?

'The Press Complaints Commission is the cornerstone of the Press's continually shaky hold on the right to self-regulation.'
Roy Greenslade, *The Guardian*

'The question of privacy and the reform of media law will not go away.'
Alastair Brett, *The Times*

Journalists are obviously answerable to their editors. But they are also – the editors, too – answerable to organisations whose specific duty is to monitor and regulate the Press and broadcasting.

The following sections look at some of the difficult areas for journalists.

Privacy and the Press

The issue of the right to privacy is very much in the public eye. In the past decade there have been a number of calls for laws to curb the power of the Press to investigate and report on the private lives or dealings of public figures. So far, no legislation has gone through and newspapers are self-regulating. They abide by a Code of Conduct laid down by the Press Complaints Commission (see pages 173–77).

The National Union of Journalists and the Chartered Institute of Journalists also have rules of conduct for their members (see pages 177–78). Some still break the rules. For example, in 1995 the editor of the *News of The World* was reprimanded by the newspaper's proprietor, Rupert Murdoch, for invading the privacy of Countess Spencer, wife of the Princess of Wales's brother, after she was photographed at a clinic.

Bias in broadcasting

Broadcast journalists must comply with the code of practice set out by the Broadcasting Standards Council which gives guidelines on violence, sex, taste and decency.

Accusations of bias are a particular problem for broadcasters. Broadcasting organisations are required by law to be impartial and balanced. While a newspaper may come out in favour of one political party, television and radio are prohibited from doing so.

During the lifetime of John Major's government, the BBC fended off several allegations of 'bias' against the Conservative party.

- The BBC was set up with a mission to 'inform, educate and entertain.' It is governed by Royal Charter and funded by the television licence fee. The government of the day has the power to stop the BBC broadcasting any programme.

- Independent television is regulated by the Independent Television Commission. It licenses stations and can intervene over lapses of impartiality, the portrayal of violence, lapses of good taste and decency. It can halt programmes which might lead to crime and disorder or be offensive to the public.

- The Radio Authority oversees independent radio stations.

How do people complain?

If someone who has been the subject of a story, feature documentary or news report feels there has been an intrusion upon their privacy or they have been treated unfairly, he or she can complain. In the case of newspapers, the complaint is to the **Press Complaints Commission**. In the case of radio and television, to the **Broadcasting Complaints Commission**.

If the complaint is upheld, an apology or retraction is likely to be published or broadcast.

The government is considering setting up a body to pay compensation to victims of newspaper intrusion, with funds coming from newspapers themselves. It is also considering outlawing the use of telephoto-lens photography and electronic eavesdropping.

Protecting sources

Journalists are often given confidential information which they then use as the basis for a story. This is usually done on the understanding that the source – the person who gave the information – will not be identified.

The sort of information given often relates to the actions of government or to large companies and organisations. For example, a government report shows that the number of unemployed school-leavers is rising rapidly. The government of the day decides to suppress the findings, because they reflect badly on its economic policies. A senior civil servant could take the view that the public has a right to know and 'leak' the report to a journalist. The journalist will not name his or her 'mole'. First, they will understand they were given the information in confidence. Second, they will not want to reveal the name of a good contact who may give them stories in the future.

Occasionally, there have been cases of a journalist being taken to court and ordered to reveal the name of a source, but such cases are rare.

Journalists' unions expect their members to respect the confidentiality of sources.

Taking 'freebies'

Journalists are often offered 'facilities' by companies and organisations. An example might be a cruise on a superb new liner. The company hopes the journalist will write or broadcast a positive view of the trip, thus generating priceless publicity.

Should journalists accept 'freebies'?

Opinion is divided. Most newspapers allow their writers to accept, but stipulate it must be made clear in the copy. In the case of a holiday, the feature would say that the journalist was travelling as a guest of so-and-so.

Some newspapers, such as *The Independent*, do not allow staff to take freebies. Journalists themselves generally feel that there is nothing wrong with accepting a freebie as long as they are then allowed to write honestly about them.

THE LAW

'Ignorance of the law excuses no man'
John Selden (1584–1654)

'Editors ... have been known to complain if they feel a rival newspaper is getting away with publishing more than they have themselves, while journalists press to include as much as can be legally got away with. But the lawyer has to stand his ground and demand balancing quotes or the deletion of unsupportable allegations.'
Duncan Lamont, *The Independent*

Journalists have no special privileges in law. They must obey the laws of the land like any other citizen.

There are, however, certain laws which particularly affect journalists. They must be vigilant about libel and court reporting. A slip up in libelling someone could cost a huge amount in damages; contempt of court might lead to an editor being summoned before a court, and even jailed.

Libel

Britain has stringent libel laws. What is a libel? It is a statement that would:

'Expose a person to hatred, ridicule or contempt, cause him to be shunned and avoided, lower him in the estimation of right thinking members of society generally, or disparage him in his office, profession or trade.'
Essential Law for Journalists, McNae

Journalists must take extreme care not to print or broadcast anything **untruthful** that could constitute a libel.

The defences to a libel case are complex; any journalist who is even slightly worried that something they wish to write or broadcast might give cause to a court action must seek advice from the legal office first.

Court reporting

There are complex laws governing what can be reported from a court case. If these laws are broken, a journalist could be found in 'contempt of court' and liable to a fine or, in an extreme case, imprisonment.

The laws are many, but here are two examples:

- Newspapers and broadcasting organisations may not identify a victim in a rape case.

- They may not report anything that went on in court while a jury was out of a courtroom.

Journalists also need to be particularly well informed of the laws governing copyright, race relations and official secrets.

THE FUTURE

'The only way the electronic media will kill newspapers is if we commit suicide.'
Chris Oakley, *Towards 2000: Newspapers and the Millennium*

'Imagine an electronic newspaper delivered to your home. Assume it is sent to a magical, paper thin, flexible, waterproof wireless, lightweight display. Imagine a future in which a computer can read every newswire and newspaper and catch every television and radio broadcast on the planet, and then construct a personalised summary – a newspaper in an edition of one.'

Nicholas Negroponte, *Being Digital*

What will life be like for the journalist of the future? Who will he or she work for? Where will the jobs be?

The media is expanding. Television, radio, newspapers and magazines all employ many more journalists than they did twenty years ago. The signs are that they will continue to grow and that journalists will be in great demand in the year 2000.

This section examines some of the changes we can expect to see.

Television

Digital broadcasting will open up the airwaves to many more 'terrestrial' channels. Britain got one such new national channel – Channel 5 – in 1997. Up to thirty other channels could follow.

There are likely to be many more cable and satellite channels too.

For example, the Mirror Group has a cable channel, Live TV, eventually intended to cover the entire UK.

They may not all need journalists, but some certainly will.

Existing television companies are also expanding their services. For example, Eurosport, the pan-European sports channel, is to begin separate national services in some countries.

Newspapers

Newspapers are healthier than they may look. Circulations of many regional and some national papers fell in the past decade. A small number of national newspapers were launched, and then closed. But new newspapers are still launched, such as *The County Standard* in Warwickshire, which first rolled off the presses in February 1995.

Newspaper publishers are moving into new areas. Some, including the *Daily Telegraph* and *Liverpool Daily Post*, have already started 'electronic' newspapers. These are on-screen versions of the printed product which can be read on the Internet, the global computer network.

The *Wall Street Journal* has gone further and will produce *The Personal Journal* for an individual reader – at a price, of course. This electronic newspaper is geared to the interests of the specific reader and is then downloaded into their personal computer.

Other newspaper publishing companies are investigating ways of becoming news providers – selling a news service as well as publishing it.

The journalists

The journalist of the year 2010 may well work for more than one medium. One journalist may go on an assignment, write their story for print, script it in a different form for radio or television and even edit a version to go out in an electronic newspaper.

Chris Oakley, chief executive of Midland Independent Newspapers, outlined a vision of the future to a conference of editors in 1995, in which he saw broadcast and print working together. It was that 'journalists will write their stories, using a portable PC, but produce a headline transcript for radio broadcast and be the talking heads on cable news. Access to the printed product will be through the newsagent, down a line, on a television and via a PC.'

9

The Way In:
Training for Journalism

'England in the year 2000 will be a nation not of shopkeepers (of course not), not of politicians (some cheer there), not of engineers (sad to tell), but of journalists.'

David Martens, *The Spectator*

BECOMING A JOURNALIST

In theory, anyone can become a journalist. If you write an article, and sell it to a magazine, you are on your way. There are no restrictions on setting up as a freelance.

In practice, the majority of journalists in Britain have undergone formal training. There are certain basics every journalist must learn, such as how to interview, how to research and the law.

Going on a training course does not guarantee you a job. Jobs in journalism are highly sought after. Most employers look for more than a completed training course. You must give yourself an edge over the other applicants.

What else do editors look for?

They will prefer the candidate who sees the 'job' as much more than a job. They will look for evidence of your enthusiasm for the media and your involvement in it. They will want to be sure you will not mind working many hours of unpaid overtime. They will also ask themselves, can she or he go out and talk to people? Is she presentable? Can he work alone?

So when you take the decision that you want to become a journalist, investigate training opportunities thoroughly. But also start to build up a portfolio of evidence of your commitment to the profession.

- Get something published or broadcast – even in your school magazine, or on hospital radio.

- Offer to work at the local newspaper or radio station in your holidays – if only as a tea boy or messenger.
- Read as many newspapers and magazines as you can, and watch news and current affairs on television.
- Get clued up about the news at home and abroad.
- Do everything you can to add to your plus points.

Getting trained

Very few young people enter journalism without completing a college course or agreeing to undergo on-the-job training. The number of media courses is growing, but competition for places is fierce. In 1995 there were 20 applicants for every place available on university courses in 'mass communications'. There are a bewildering number of routes into journalism, and it is necessary to look at all the options in order to make an informed choice.

You will need to identify which section of the media you want to work in – newspapers, magazines, books, radio, television, public relations – as training is increasingly geared to specific jobs. There has been a sea change in the recruitment of trainees in the past two decades. Journalism was once a profession dedicated to 'on-the-job' training and putting great value on experience. Now, new entrants are far more likely to be graduates, a trend that seems certain to continue.

The National Council for the Training of Journalists awards the **National Certificate** in newspaper journalism. Its minimum standard is five GCSE passes (grades A–C) or equivalent. But it points out: 'In recent years it has become rare for a trainee to come into the industry at this level. Over half the recruits are university graduates and many of the others have achieved at least two A-levels or equivalent.'

Where can you get training?

For those not in employment, a growing number of colleges and universities offer media courses. Privately run training centres are also booming, offering short courses in specific areas, such as sub-editing or documentary film making.

For those who have gained a job as a junior writer or reporter, there are colleges and in-company training centres.

Starting out in newspapers

There are a number of different ways to begin a career in print journalism. Most people get their first job on a provincial newspaper. After leaving school you can:

- Apply direct to local newspapers.
- Apply for a pre-entry course, usually lasting one year.
- Apply to do a degree in journalism.

Graduates in subjects other than media can:

- Apply direct to newspapers.
- Do a postgraduate degree in journalism.

When you join a newspaper as a junior reporter you will usually work towards a formal qualification, either the **National Certificate** awarded by the NCTJ or **National Vocational Qualifications** (NVQs), awarded by various bodies.

At present, newspaper journalism training is split between that controlled by the NCTJ and that controlled by newspaper groups. These are the main ways of getting in:

1. Provincial newspaper trainees

Trainees find a job with a local paper direct from school or university.

The first six months is likely to be 'probationary' and you are likely to enter into a two-year training contract. At first, you will probably be given a distance learning pack. Once your probation is over, you will start your training proper.

Training is usually in the form of short courses or periods of block release. The rest of the time, you continue your job as a junior reporter.

Some provincial newspaper groups arrange training through the NCTJ, with block release at accredited colleges. Others have in-company training centres, and their schemes lead to NVQs. You will be expected to obtain the National Certificate or NVQs at Level 4.

How to apply: Directly to the editors of your chosen papers which you can find in a media directory such as *Benn's UK Media Directory* or *Willing's Press Guide*.

2. Pre-entry courses

This is a full-time course at a college of further or higher education which you take before starting work. You must have at least two A-levels. Some colleges will expect you to have done a short period of work experience.

After completing your pre-entry course, you still have to find a job. Once you begin work, you are likely to do three months probation and enter into an 18-month training contract. You will be expected to obtain the National Certificate or NVQs.

How to apply: For pre-entry courses, apply through the NCTJ.

3. Taking a journalism degree

There are courses for both school-leavers and graduates. These can be found in general guides to university courses. Once you have graduated, you must take your chances in the job market. You can apply to become a trainee on a provincial newspaper, or for one of the very few graduate traineeships on national newspapers.

How to apply: Direct to the university/through the Universities and Colleges Admission Service (UCAS).

4. National newspaper trainees

The opportunities are few and far between. Some national newspapers offer traineeships but almost all are for graduates. Opportunities vary from year to year. They are usually advertised in *The Guardian* media section or in the *UK Press Gazette*.

How to apply: Contact the newspapers direct for information.

The over-30s

If you are over 30, it is still possible to begin a career in print journalism. Some people decide to set up as a freelance and take short courses offered by various training establishments. These are advertised in *The Guardian* media section, but always make sure they are accredited by either the NCTJ or the NUJ. Any worthwhile journalism training will cover journalism practice, government, law, and shorthand.

Some may still get jobs in provincial or national newspapers. Approach the editor direct, making a clear case of why he or she should take you on.

Getting a foothold in magazines

If you are a school-leaver, you have the following options:

- You can apply direct to the magazines of your choice.
- You can go on to further education, taking courses in periodical

journalism. There are both diplomas and postgraduate courses. If you complete one of these, you then apply direct to editors. As with newspapers, the trend is towards graduate recruitment.

- A school-leaver with A-levels may still be able to get a job. In this case, you will probably be trained on short courses run by the Periodicals Training Council.
- Some companies run their own training schemes, but the situation changes from year to year. You will normally obtain NVQs in one or more of these subjects: news writing, feature writing, subbing, and subbing with layout.

What are the minimum qualifications?
There is no industry standard but one A-level is usually the minimum. However, around 85 per cent of recruits to magazine journalism are graduates. Specialist knowledge or an appropriate degree might help you to get a job on a relevant title.

Are jobs advertised?
Some are, especially on the lower rungs of the ladder. Again, read the media section of *The Guardian* and the *UK Press Gazette*.

Freelances
As with newspapers, you can try freelancing. In this case you would need either a diploma/degree in periodical journalism, or you would need to take courses at one of the private training centres in such subjects as feature writing.

Beginning in broadcasting
Many journalists in radio and television are experienced and have moved across from newspapers. But it is possible to start out in broadcasting.

What do you do after leaving school?
- You can apply direct to radio and television organisations, for a place on a company training scheme.
- You can apply for pre-entry courses in broadcast journalism. These are on offer at colleges around Britain. Pre-entry courses are also run for graduates. Completing a pre-entry course does not guarantee you a job, but because competition is so fierce it is a distinct advantage.
- Or you can apply to take a full, three-year degree.

Any course is likely to cover the following:
- Theory and practice of broadcast journalism.
- Technical skills and practical training in news writing and editing.
- Bulletin preparation, interviewing techniques and the ability to communicate effectively.
- Law, public administration, ethics and media studies.
- Check that any course you apply for is approved by the National Council for the Training of Broadcast Journalists.

Working for the BBC

Many journalists want to work for the BBC, described by the director general, John Birt, as 'the most powerful journalistic enterprise in the world.'

The corporation employs 700 journalists but takes on only a few trainees each year and competition is intense. Its News Trainee Scheme recruits about 12 people a year for two-year training in television and radio. Applicants are usually aged 21 to 25 and are graduates, with some work experience.

It also operates a local radio trainee reporter scheme: this offers fewer than 40 places a year on a 20-month scheme for applicants aged 20 to 30 with at least A-levels. The scheme excludes trained journalists.

Independent television and radio

ITN (Independent Television News) and some regional television companies also recruit a small number of graduates; again, opportunities vary from year to year, so write to the television companies for the latest information.

Independent radio organisations run varying in-company training schemes; contact your preferred stations direct. Broadcasters are listed in *The Writer's Handbook*.

A career in public relations

Many jobs in public relations are filled by journalists with no formal experience of PR. Most, however, will have an awareness of what public relations officers do, having dealt with them on a day-to-day basis.

There are two choices for the school-leaver: apply to be taken on by a PR company, or apply to take a course with a PR element.

Some PR companies have in-house training for graduates. Most work towards the Communication, Advertising and Marketing

Education Foundation diploma or certificate (CAM). Subjects covered for the **certificate** are marketing, advertising, public relations, media, research and behavioural studies, sales promotion and direct marketing.

The **diploma** covers management and strategy, public relations management, public relations practice, consumer advertising, business-to-business advertising, international advertising, sales promotion management and structure, sales promotion practice and direct marketing.

What qualifications do you need?

To take the certificate you must be at least 18 and (i) have a degree or (ii) two A-levels plus three O-levels, or (iii) five GCSE passes at grade C or above. Those with the certificate, or equivalent, can take the diploma.

Otherwise, there are various courses with a public relations element. Communications studies, media studies or business studies courses often contain a PR module. The syllabus is set by the Institute of Public Relations or the Public Relations Consultants Association. Postgraduate degrees and part-time diplomas are also on offer.

Getting into book publishing

Publishers recruit both school-leavers with good A-levels and graduates. Write direct to the publishing company in which you have an interest.

The **Book House Training Centre** is the largest provider of courses for the book and journal publishing industry. It offers courses leading to NVQs, for both publishing employees and freelances. These include copy book editing, book production, book commissioning and journal production editing. It also runs short courses including copy editing and proof reading, commissioning and many others.

APPLYING FOR A JOB

'Remember that the interviewer is trying to establish two things: if you can do the job and just as important, whether you are the kind of person that they want.'

A Career in Magazines,
Periodical Publishers Association

Room 24
Shire Buildings
University of Westland
Seafront Road
Westland
Westshire

Ms Patricia Vincent
Editor
Westland Evening Times

11 March 199X

Dear Ms Vincent

I am writing to ask you to consider employing me as a trainee reporter.

I am at present working towards a BA in Media Studies and will complete my degree in July. I am determined on a career in journalism and believe I have the enthusiasm and the personal qualities to succeed.

I have been editing my university newspaper for the past year and have had a feature article about student life published in the Westshire Times. I have also had two letters published in *The Guardian*.

I am an outgoing person, have a positive approach, am not afraid of working long hours and understand that journalism is not always a glamorous job. I would be keen to come into the newspaper during my half-term break in April, and would be happy to work at whatever would be useful.

I enclose a separate sheet showing my educational qualifications and work experience.

Yours sincerely

Sean O'Riordan

Fig. 14. Writing a job application.

When you are ready to apply for jobs, you can either:

- Write direct to editors of publications or organisations.
- Reply to job advertisements.

One of the best sources of advertisements for jobs and graduate traineeships is the *UK Press Gazette*, published weekly on Thursday. You can buy this in some newsagents' shops in London or on subscription. The other source is *The Guardian* media section, published on Saturday and Monday. *The Times* and *The Independent* each have media pages, but they carry fewer opportunities.

Writing the letter

When you write to an editor **on spec** remember that he or she probably gets many similar letters. Make yours distinctive, say why you want to join the publication or broadcast organisation and list the reasons why they should take you on. Type it, or get it typed professionally. The letter should be concise, with your CV on a separate sheet (see example in Figure 14).

When you are **replying to an advertisement** for a specific job, target your letter at that job. Explain your strengths in relation to it, say why you would like to do it and explain how your own experience is relevant to it.

Keep letters to editors reasonably brief. Always address the editor by name, check the spelling and be sure that you have got his or her title (Mr, Sir, Ms) right.

What do you do if you don't get a reply?

Wait at least ten days or so; editors are extremely busy people. Then telephone his or her secretary and make sure your letter was received; if so, ask politely if the editor has seen it and when you can expect a reply. You may find it has gone astray in a mountain of internal mail; if so, send a copy.

If you do not receive a reply within a couple of weeks, ring again. Ask the secretary if she could draw your letter to the editor's attention.

What happens when you get an interview?

The key to success is being prepared. Take these few simple steps:

1. Research the organisation's background. Find out what it publishes or broadcasts and which other companies it is linked with.

2. Find out as much as you can about the editors and the senior journalists. You may be facing a panel of them at your interview.
3. See if you can spend a day in the newsroom or with a reporter. Write to the news editor explaining that you are hoping to become a journalist.
4. Be well informed about recent news events when you go for your interview.
5. Think through some of the questions you may be asked, and your answers. For example: 'Why do you want to become a journalist?' Know your reasons.
6. Take with you evidence of any relevant work experience – copies of the university newspaper, or a letter from a newspaper or radio station you spent a day with.
7. Think of the questions you want to ask. For example: what training will I get? Will I be able to fulfil a special interest, such as football reporting?

A selection of job advertisements

Regional television company: Has a vacancy for a journalist to write and present news bulletins and to present for the nightly news magazine programme. Contract position. Experienced journalists, preferably with local radio experience, should apply. Please send CV, together with a colour photograph or video showreel.

Radio journalists: This station has an unrivalled reputation for breaking stories and developing them fully in bulletins, sequences and debates. The position calls for a journalist who will originate ideas and treatments suitable for a station that sets the local news agenda. A wide general knowledge, good broadcasting voice, precision writing and ambitions to produce sequences and documentaries are essential.

Freelance editor: Opportunity for an established freelance journalist with a proven track record to assume responsibility for editing this monthly journal. The successful applicant will be required to produce investigative features, reports and case studies, to commission features from experts in the field, to handle copy from first draft to final proof and to maintain the journal's existing high profile. Fees negotiable.

Magazine chief sub-editor: A bright, busy, breezy monthly needs a fast, accurate, lively chief sub who can chase and sharpen copy with equal ease. Experience of Apple Mac essential. Sense of humour an advantage. Send CV with covering letter.

Press and public relations manager: Our growing Press and PR function plays a key role in the promotion of our products and our company. For the new Press and PR manager we seek, there is the scope to provide strategic leadership on all internal and external Press and PR issues, as well as manage our PR agency and liaise extensively with both senior journalists and management. To succeed in this diverse and challenging role, you will need at least three years' experience in Press and PR, supported by a solid journalistic background. Stamina, commitment and the ability to influence and persuade decision-makers at all levels are essential. Write for more information and an application form.

Local radio: Senior journalist to help run the newsroom as morning editor. Radio experience needed.

Quark sub wanted: Weekly newspaper is looking for an experienced, creative senior sub-editor to produce news and feature pages. Working knowledge of QuarkXpress essential. Apply in writing, with CV.

Features deputy: Top selling tabloid has a great opportunity for an experienced features executive. Must have good Mac skills, lots of energy and big ideas. Salary up to £40,000.

Evening newspaper: Senior reporters and photographers. We need top flight reporters, including an education specialist, to join our team of professionals on this big selling evening newspaper. You will need boundless energy, enthusiasm, commitment and ideas to join a paper which is going places after a relaunch and redesign. We offer state of the art technology. Apply, with the best examples of your recent work.

SALARIES

'Most of us could use a rise.'

Supplement to *The Journalist*

The wages of journalism can range from less than £10,000 pa on a weekly newspaper to more than £100,000 pa for a top, national newspaper columnist. Salaries of £250,000 are sometimes reported for television presenters.

Here are some typical salaries for experienced journalists:

- Press and public relations officer, London: £21,500–£25,600.
- Reporter for aviation magazine: £17,000 pa.
- Radio newsroom journalists: £18,738–£25,651, plus £3,272 unpredictability allowance.

- Editor for monthly magazine, members' newsletter and weekly news sheet: £24,000.
- Editor, modern language books: £16,000–£20,000 pa.
- Senior broadcast journalists: £21,003–£32,429, plus £3,272 unpredictability allowance.
- Night editor, national newspaper: £60,000 plus.
- Trainee journalists may expect to start on something between £10,000 and £17,000, depending on qualifications and on who they are working for. For example, the BBC pays its news trainees £12,500 pa, ITN £17,000.

In a salary survey in 1995, the NUJ found that of under-25s:

- The largest group earned £10,000–£15,000.
- Next largest was £15,000–£19,000.
- The third largest group earned less than £10,000.
- Few earned over £25,000.

The same survey found that:

- One in ten of *NUJ members* who responded earned less than £10,000 pa, but almost 8 per cent earned more than £40,000 pa.
- *In national newspapers*: two-thirds of journalists earned £30,000 or more.
- *In provincial papers*: only 2.1 per cent of members earned more than £30,000.
- *National agencies*: staff working for national agencies earned between £20,000 and £30,000.
- *National television*: staff pay was slightly less than national newspapers.
- *Regional TV*: most earnings were between £20,000 and £35,000.
- *National radio*: earnings closely reflected those in regional TV.
- *Local and regional radio*: earnings were well below those for national radio.
- *Magazines*: most journalists earned £15,000 to £25,000.
- *Books*: most members earned £10,000 to £30,000.
- *Public relations*: two-thirds earned between £15,000 and £30,000.

Appendix: Codes of Practice

THE PRESS COMPLAINTS COMMISSION CODE OF PRACTICE

All members of the Press have a duty to maintain the highest professional and ethical standards. In doing so, they should have regard to the provisions of this Code of Practice and to safeguarding the public's right to know.

Editors are responsible for the actions of journalists employed by their publications. They should also satisfy themselves as far as possible that material accepted from non-staff members was obtained in accordance with this Code.

While recognising that this involves a substantial element of self-restraint by editors and journalists, it is designed to be acceptable in the context of a system of self-regulation. The Code applies in the spirit as well as in the letter.

It is the responsibility of editors to co-operate as swiftly as possible with PCC enquiries.

Any publication which is criticised by the PCC under one of the following clauses is duty bound to print the adjudication which follows in full and with due prominence.

1. Accuracy

i.   Newspapers and periodicals should take care not to publish inaccurate, misleading or distorted material.
ii. Whenever it is recognised that a significant inaccuracy, misleading statement or distorted report has been published, it should be corrected promptly and with due prominence.
iii. An apology should be published whenever appropriate.
iv. A newspaper or periodical should always report fairly and accurately the outcome for an action of defamation to which it has been a party.

2. Opportunity to reply
A fair opportunity for reply to inaccuracies should be given to individuals or organisations when reasonably called for.

3. Comment, conjecture and fact
Newspapers, whilst free to be partisan, should distinguish clearly between comment, conjecture and fact.

4. Privacy
Intrusions and enquiries into an individual's private life without his or her consent, including the use of long-lens photography to take pictures of people on private property without their consent, are not generally acceptable and publication can only be justified when in the public interest.
Note: private property is defined as any private residence, together with its garden and outbuildings, but excluding any adjacent fields or parkland. In addition, hotel bedrooms (but not other areas in a hotel) and those parts of a hospital or nursing home where patients are treated or accommodated.

5. Listening devices
Unless justified by public interest, journalists should not obtain or publish material obtained by using clandestine listening devices or by intercepting private telephone conversations.

6. Hospitals
i.   Journalists or photographers making enquiries at hospitals or similar institutions should identify themselves to a responsible executive and obtain permission before entering non-public areas.
ii. The restrictions on intruding into privacy are particularly relevant to enquiries about individuals in hospitals or similar institutions.

7. Misrepresentation
i.   Journalists should not generally obtain or seek to obtain information or pictures through misrepresentation or subterfuge.
ii. Unless in the public interest, documents or photographs should be removed only with the express consent of the owner.
iii. Subterfuge can be justified only in the public interest and only

when material cannot be obtained by any other means.

8. Harassment

i. Journalists should neither obtain nor seek to obtain information or pictures through intimidation or harassment.
ii. Unless their enquiries are in the public interest, journalists should not photograph individuals on private property (as defined in the note to Clause 4) without their consent; should not persist in telephoning or questioning individuals after having been asked to desist; should not remain on their property after having been asked to leave and should not follow them.
iii. It is the responsibility of editors to ensure that these requirements are carried out.

9. Payment for articles

Payment or offers of payment for stories, pictures or information should not be made directly or through agents to witnesses or potential witnesses in current criminal proceedings or to people engaged in crime or their associates – which includes family, friends, neighbours and colleagues – except where the material concerned ought to be published in the public interest and the payment is necessary for this to be done.

10. Intrusion into grief and shock

In cases involving personal grief or shock, enquiries should be carried out and approaches made with sympathy and discretion.

11. Innocent relatives and friends

Unless it is contrary to the public's right to know, the Press should generally avoid identifying relatives or friends of persons convicted or accused of crime.

12. Interviewing or photographing children

i. Journalists should not normally interview or photograph children under the age of 16 on subjects involving the personal welfare of the child in the absence of or without the consent of a parent or other adult who is responsible for the children.
ii. Children should not be approached or photographed while at school without the permission of the school authorities.

13. Children in sex cases

(1) The Press should not, even where the law does not prohibit it, identify children under the age of 16 who are involved in cases concerning sexual offences, whether as victims, or as witnesses or defendants.

(2) In any press report of a case involving a sexual offence against a child:

i.   The adult should be identified.

ii.   The term 'incest' where applicable should not be used.

iii. The offence should be described as 'serious offences against young children' or similar appropriate wording.

iv.   The child should not be identified.

v.   Care should be taken that nothing in the report implies the relationship between the accused and the child.

14. Victims of crime

The Press should not identify victims of sexual assault or publish material likely to contribute to such identification unless, by law, they are free to do so.

15. Discrimination

i.   The press should avoid prejudicial or pejorative reference to a person's race, colour, religion, sex or sexual orientation or to any physical or mental illness or handicap.

ii.   It should avoid publishing details of a person's race, colour, religion, sex or sexual orientation, unless these are directly relevant to the story.

16. Financial journalism

i.   Even where the law does not prohibit it, journalists should not use for their own profit financial information they receive in advance of its general publication, nor should they pass such information to others.

ii.   They should not write about shares or securities in whose performance they know that they or their close families have a significant financial interest, without disclosing the interest to the editor or the financial editor.

iii. They should not buy or sell, either directly or through nominees or agents, shares or securities about which they have written recently, or about which they intend to write in the near future.

17. Confidential sources
Journalists have a moral obligation to protect confidential sources of information.

18. The public interest
Clauses 4, 5, 7, 8 and 9 create exceptions which may be covered by invoking the public interest. For the purposes of this Code, that is most easily defined as:

i.   Detecting or exposing crime or a serious misdemeanour.
ii. Protecting public health and safety.
iii. Preventing the public from being misled by some statement or action of an individual or organisation.

In any cases raising issues beyond these three definitions, the Press Complaints Commission will require a full explanation by the editor of the publication involved, seeking to demonstrate how the public interest was served.

October 1994

NATIONAL UNION OF JOURNALISTS' CODE OF CONDUCT

1. A journalist has a duty to maintain the highest professional and ethical standards.
2. A journalist shall at all times defend the principle of the freedom of the Press and other media in relation to the collection of information and the expression of comment and criticism. He/she shall strive to eliminate distortion, news suppression and censorship.
3. A journalist shall strive to ensure that the information he/she disseminates is fair and accurate, avoid the expression of comment and conjecture as established fact and falsification by distortion, selection or misrepresentation.
4. A journalist shall rectify promptly any harmful inaccuracies, ensure that correction and apologies receive due prominence and afford the right of reply to persons criticised when the issue is of sufficient importance.
5. A journalist shall obtain information, photographs and illustrations only by straightforward means. The use of other means can be justified only by overriding considerations of the

public interest. The journalist is entitled to exercise a personal conscientious objection to the use of such means.

6. Subject to the justification by overriding considerations of the public interest, a journalist shall do nothing which entails intrusion into private grief and distress.

7. A journalist shall protect confidential sources of information.

8. A journalist shall not accept bribes nor shall he/she allow other inducements to influence the performance of his/her professional duties.

9. A journalist shall not lend himself/herself to the distortion or suppression of the truth because of advertising or other considerations.

10. A journalist shall only mention a person's race, colour, creed, illegitimacy, disability, marital status (or lack of it), gender or sexual orientation if this information is strictly relevant. A journalist shall neither originate nor process material which encourages discrimination on any of the above-mentioned grounds.

11. A journalist shall not take private advantage of information gained in the course of his/her duties, before the information is public knowledge.

12. A journalist shall not, by way of statement, voice or appearance endorse by advertisement any commercial product or service save for the promotion of his/her own work or of the medium by which he/she is employed.

Sources of Further Information

'If you want to make a fortune, don't work on a newspaper; own it.'

James Cameron

It is impossible to list every course in journalism or media studies, not least because they change from year to year. What follows will point you in the right direction to get the detailed information you require.

HOW DO I FIND OUT MORE?

For training information, contact the following:

Newspapers
- National Council for the Training of Journalists, Latton Bush Centre, Southern Way, Harlow, Essex CM18 7BL.

Broadcasting
- National Council for the Training of Broadcast Journalists, 188 Lichfield Court, Sheen Road, Richmond TW9 1BB.
- ITN, 200 Gray's Inn Road, London WC1X 8XZ.
- BBC (radio), Broadcasting House, London W1A 1AA.
- BBC (television), Television Centre, Wood Lane, London W12 7RJ.
- Association of Independent Radio Companies, Radio House, 46 Westbourne Grove, London W2 5SH.
- ITV Association, Knighton House, 56 Mortimer Street, London WIN 8AN.

Magazines
- Periodical Publishers Association, Imperial House, 15-19 Kingsway, London WC2B 6UN.
- Periodicals Training Council at the address above.

Books
- Book House Training Centre, 45 East Hill, Wandsworth, London SW18 2QZ.

Public relations
- Institute of Public Relations, 15 Northburgh Street, London EC1V OPR.
- CAM (Communication, Advertising and Marketing Education Foundation), Abford House, 15 Wilton Road, London SW1V 1NJ.
- Government Information Service, Marketing, Recruitment and Training Division, Information Officer Management Unit, Cabinet Office, Horse Guards Road, London SW1P 3AL.

Can I join any organisations?
Unions may accept student members:

- British Association of Journalists, 88 Fleet Street, London EC4Y 1PJ.
- National Union of Journalists, Acorn House, 314-320 Gray's Inn Road, London WC1X 8DP.
- Chartered Institute of Journalists, 2 Dock Offices, Surrey Quays Road, London SE16 2XU.

How can I learn more about journalism practice?
There are a number of good journalism manuals, for example:

Journalism for Beginners, Joan Clayton (Piatkus).
Teach Yourself Journalism, Michael Bromely (Hodder & Stoughton).
Broadcast Journalism, Andrew Boyd (Focal Press).
McNae's Essential Law for Journalists, Tom Welsh and Walter Greenwood (Butterworths).

Which newspapers and journals carry media news and job advertisements?
The best are *The Guardian* media section and the *UK Press Gazette*, followed by the media pages in *The Times* and *The Independent*. See also *Campaign, Broadcast, PR Week, Media Week* and *The Bookseller*.

COURSES IN THE MEDIA

How do I choose a course?
Discuss which course is best for you with your careers adviser. Basic information on courses is found in:

- *Media Courses in Britain*, The British Council, Medlock Street, Manchester M15 4PR. Gives details of training courses in broadcast journalism. Enquiries to Senior Media Adviser, Education Department.

- *Media Courses UK*, edited by Lavinia Orton (BFI Publishing). Includes courses at further and higher education level.

- *Which Degree in Britain*, Careers Research and Advisory Council (Hobson). Undergraduate courses. CRAC also publishes a guide to postgraduate courses.

Or you can write to or telephone colleges and universities direct. The lists below give a guide to centres of training, but are not exhaustive.

When you are thinking of applying for courses, try to aim for those which are accredited by the training organisations.

Courses recognised by the NCTBJ or seeking recognition
Bell College of Technology, Hamilton.
Bournemouth University.
City University, London.
Darlington College of Technology.
Falmouth School of Art & Design.
Goldsmith's College, University of London.
Highbury College of Technology, Portsmouth.
London College of Printing.
University of Central England in Birmingham.
University of Central Lancashire.
Nottingham Trent University.
Sunderland University.
Northern Media School, Sheffield Hallam University.
Trinity and All Saints College, University of Leeds.
Surrey Institute of Art & Design.
University of Wales.
University of Westminster.

Vauxhall College, London.

NCTJ accredited courses
Bell College of Technology, Hamilton.
Calderdale College, Halifax.
City of Liverpool Community College.
City University, London.
Cornwall College.
Darlington College of Technology.
Gloucestershire College of Arts & Technology.
Gwent Tertiary College.
Harlow College.
Highbury College.
Lambeth College.
Napier University Edinburgh.
Sheffield College.
Strathclyde University.
Surrey Institute of Art & Design.
University of Central Lancashire.
University of Wales.
Yale College, Wrexham.

Courses in magazine journalism
University of Wales.
City University, London.
London College of Printing.
Highbury College.
The London College of Fashion.

Public relations courses
CAM courses are on offer at colleges around the country. Students must register with CAM before starting a course. Distance learning courses are also available. Undergraduate and/or postgraduate courses:

Bournemouth University.
Leeds Metropolitan University.
College of St Mark and St John, Plymouth.
Cranfield School of Management.
Stirling University.

Courses in book publishing

Undergraduate and/or postgraduate:

Middlesex University.
London College of Printing.
Exeter University.
Napier University, Edinburgh.
Oxford Brookes University.
Reading University.
Stirling University.
West London Institute.

Applying for jobs and traineeships: how do I find them?

If you want to apply direct for a job as a junior reporter, write to the newspaper, periodical or broadcast organisation of your choice. You can find their names and addresses in:

The Writer's Handbook (Macmillan Press).
Artists' and Writers' Yearbook (A&C Black).
Willing's Press Guide.
Benn's UK Media Directory.

Glossary

In journalism, you will find an unfamiliar language. Much of it dates from the days of 'hot metal' – the pre-computer age printing process. Some of it comes from the technical side of broadcasting. Here is a guide to some of the terms you will come across.

Actuality. Recording or videotape of people or events.

Ad. Advertisement.

Backbench. Team of senior journalists who plan a newspaper.

Blurb. Artwork advertising something within a newspaper, usually on page one.

Breaking story. News event happening at present.

Bulletin. News broadcast, usually short.

Byline. Reporter's name, usually at start of a news report or feature.

Check calls. Regular calls to emergency services to find out if any news stories have broken.

Contact. Person who is a source of news information.

Copy. News reports or features, usually written and read on computer.

Correspondent. Journalist covering a specialist subject or area.

Current affairs. Feature material on television and radio.

Deadline. The time by which copy, pages or videotape editing must be complete.

Editor. The boss.

Embargo. Time or date when information can be released.

Feature. Newspaper article longer and more analytical than a news report.

Flatplan. In magazines, plan showing number of pages and position of advertisements.

Freelance. Self-employed journalist.

Headline. The heading to copy.

Intro. First paragraph of a news report or feature.

Layout. Design for newspaper or magazine page.

Leader. A newspaper's editorial comment column.

Nibs. Small news stories, also called briefs.

Package. In broadcasting, a complete story containing a journalist's report and actuality.

Pagination. Number of pages.

Press release. Publicity handout from an organisation, often embargoed.

Producer. In broadcasting, person who processes news.

Proof. Early printout of a newspaper or magazine page.

Running order. In broadcasting, a list of news items in order of importance.

Rushes. Unedited film.

Script. Another name for copy, used in television and radio.

Splash. Main story on page one of a newspaper.

Subdeck. Smaller secondary headline.

Sub-editing. Checking and cutting copy or tape.

Text. Copy once it is set in type.

Track. Soundtrack.

Vox pop. Random street interviews.

VT. Videotape, used in television news.

Index